CHRISTIANS ONLY

A Da Capo Press Reprint Series

CIVIL LIBERTIES IN AMERICAN HISTORY

GENERAL EDITOR: LEONARD W. LEVY

Claremont Graduate School

CHRISTIANS ONLY

A Study in Prejudice

By

HEYWOOD BROUN

& GEORGE BRITT

DA CAPO PRESS • NEW YORK • 1974

Library of Congress Cataloging in Publication Data

Broun, Heywood Campbell, 1888-1939.
Christians only; a study in prejudice.

(Civil liberties in American history)
Reprint of the ed. published by Vanguard Press, New York.
1. Antisemitism — United States. I. Britt, George, 1895- joint author. II. Title. III. Series.
DS146.U6B76 1974 301.45′19′24073 73-19688
ISBN 0-306-70599-0

This Da Capo Press edition of *Christians Only* is an unabridged republication of the first edition published in New York in 1931

Published by Da Capo Press, Inc.
A Subsidiary of Plenum Publishing Corporation
227 West 17th Street, New York, N.Y. 10011

Manufactured in the United States of America

CHRISTIANS ONLY

CHRISTIANS ONLY

A Study in Prejudice

By

HEYWOOD BROUN

& GEORGE BRITT

THE VANGUARD PRESS · NEW YORK

MANUFACTURED IN THE UNITED STATES OF AMERICA
BY THE H. WOLFF ESTATE

Thanks

The Jewish editor of *The Day* in New York recently quoted the hostile definition: "A book is something which one Jew copies from the other." The authors of this book do not qualify for the first part of that phrase. But they must acknowledge the great extent to which they have copied, borrowed and received the benefit of the knowledge of others, particularly of Jews, in the course of gathering the material here presented. But for the suggestion and information of hundreds of friendly people, it could never have been written. These cannot be held in any way responsible for the use made of the facts or for the conclusions here drawn. But to how much of this book can they say, "I told you so"! Singling out a few among so many must seem an ungrateful forgetfulness of others. But in sincere appreciation to them all, the authors wish to give credit for help particularly to Rabbi Stephen S. Wise, Rabbi J. X. Cohen, Dr. Joshua Bloch, Dr. Jesse G. M. Bullowa, Professor Frank Gavin, Morris L. Ernst, Harry Schneiderman, Bernard G. Richards, Dr. Isaac Landman, Harold Riegelman, Bernard Postal, Isidore Sobeloff, Thomas L. Stix, Nels Anderson, Dr. A. J. Rongy, Dr. Milton Kissin, Michael Blankfort, Sidney Wallack, Edward S. Silver, Elias A. Cohen, Max J. Kohler, Dr. Morton Gottschall, and B. C. Vladeck.

CONTENTS

CHRISTIANS ONLY

Chapter I

"SHEENY"

IRVING COHEN was a sheeny and Monte Jacobs was a Jew. This classification was not my own, but that which was handed to me by the other boys on the block when I was five years old. We played on Eighty-seventh Street between Amsterdam and Columbus Avenues. This was a brownstone block, pretty far uptown in those days, for I am speaking of the year 1893 or thereabouts. We were the children of moderately prosperous middle-class American families. The avenues which bounded our territorial playground contained cheap apartment houses and the boys who come from these alien, though neighboring, abodes were very apt to be sheenies. It is my recollection, then, that my earliest lessons in prejudice were based for the most part on an economic issue and one more subtle. Since the gangs of the avenue were more numerous than our own and decidedly to be feared, it became necessary to invent some insulting epithet to hurl at them behind their backs. We could not lick them in fair fight and so we atoned for our lack of power by calling names.

But, as I have suggested, there was still another, and a more subtle, phase in prejudice. Geographically, Irving Cohen belonged to us and yet he was not admitted fully into the games of the block. The ban was not complete. If the nucleus for Red Rover, Prisoner's Base, or One Foot Off happened to be large enough, one of the older boys would tell Irving to run along. There wasn't room for anybody else to play. But when a quorum was lacking Irving could get in, and, once in, everybody tried to make him "it" and keep him that way. Irving was a sheeny and in the beginning that word sheeny meant to me no more than somebody whom you didn't like for whatever reason, explicable or otherwise. When you were very mad at anybody you called him "sheeny" just as a fighting word to get things started. Even Monte Jacobs on occasion referred to Irving as a sheeny. I can't remember that Monte was ever barred from anything. He was just about the most popular boy on the block because he was the best at games and had taken boxing lessons in a gymnasium. But I do remember hearing some parent say that it was too bad Monte was a Jew because he was such a nice boy and had such good manners.

I have no recollection of any early animosity against Jews through being told that Jews killed Christ. It is not my recollection that the matter came up during my fairly regular and compulsory attendance at an Episcopal Sunday School. The matter may have been mentioned, but I doubt that it was stressed. I have forgotten, which is, of course, no proof that something may not have come out of religion which would serve to establish prejudice. I have a feeling that it would be a decidedly interesting experiment to psycho-analyze a dozen gentiles with strongly developed anti-Jewish prejudice. It is my notion that in a great many cases the whole structure would be found to depend upon some trivial childhood incident, not infrequently a Sunday School incident. I do know that my son at the age of five years and a few months announced that he couldn't play with Miriam any more because Miriam was a Jew. When asked what that had to do with it, he told us, as if it were a headline in the latest tabloid, that "The Jews killed Christ." This, to be sure, did not represent any original research on his own part. He had merely picked up a tag out of the mouth of some playmate.

Children have a number of mean and savage instincts and they enjoy banding together against some minority in the group. If they can invent a moral reason for doing this, so much the better. Then they have the fun of the cruelty without any accompanying sense of guilt. Later on, there will be some discussion as to the real reasons for prejudice, as far as they may be ascertained, and the reasons which people are likely to give. A gap exists. The underlying motive is likely to be almost completely buried.

This can be either through design or ignorance. In the case of my son, his parents undertook, with not too gentle jest, to shame him out of his mock concern for long ago events not accurately established in his mind.

In so far as any religious prejudice existed in my own mind as a child, it was distinctly one based upon envy. At about the age of seven or eight, Irving Cohen began lording it over me by explaining that the Jews were God's chosen people. This I resented. I blamed the Jews with some nameless feeling that they must have put over the arrangement by some sort of fraud and trickery. I knew to my disturbance that there was something in what Irving said. I, too, had been to Sunday School and had heard of God's choice. Indeed, most of the early instruction was in regard to Old Testament figures who in many cases shaped up heroically. It is rather hard to blame Jewish prejudice upon instruction in the Christian Sunday School. Or at any rate, such classes can be handled in such a way as to instill no prejudice.

Yet, so treacherous and insidious is the course of prejudice that it may creep in from sources extremely difficult to identify. I would like to classify myself as civilized and yet it would be false to say that I am wholly without race or religious prejudice. Upon sudden provocation I have caught myself breaking out with all the violence of a Bassanio. The instances are not frequent but let us assume a hot day in a crowded subway car. I am just about to get out at a station when a man in an overwhelming hurry to get on tilts full against me. To my shame I must confess that at least three times in the last ten years I have turned upon him fiercely crying out, "What's your rush, you dirty kike!" It is, of course, a reproduction of a childish pattern. Once again, I am retrogressing to the old days when a "sheeny" was anyone you didn't like. The subway offender in many cases was probably more purely gentile than myself. That did not concern me. I merely reached for the most handy and deeply ingrained epithet.

School is a fertile breeding ground for discrimination. If the pupil can catch any hint of prejudice upon the part of the teacher toward so much as a single Jew in the class, the gentile child will be reassured in his own passion to haze and tease. There is no point in minimizing prejudice. It is, unfortunately, a natural impulse. I don't mean that it inevitably turns against the Jew. But every individual desires a whipping boy, and he will avail himself of whatever opportunity arises.

Already I have betrayed the muddiness of my own thinking, the manner in which my judgment and feeling have been impaired. There in the preceding paragraph you will find the telltale phrase—"the Jew". I think this particular locution has done incalculable damage in breaking down the effort of the world to achieve fraternity. I have said that prejudice is a natural instinct and I believe that; but so is fellowship. Humanity is compounded out of conflicting impulses. To write or say or even think "the Jew" is to picture the members of that community as all standardized after the manner of Ford automobiles. And, for the most part, the stencil which comes to mind is that of some gross caricature upon the stage or in a comic paper. It is this sort of thing which leads a man to say "The Jews are ill mannered." What he really means is that he once met a certain Jew whose manners did not appeal to him. Obviously, the objector has not met more than a small proportion of the Jews in the world. He is willing to generalize upon a small number of experiences.

To speak of "the Jew" is to overlook the fact that in the city of New York the variation in the group is enormous. Indeed, I think it would be accurate to say that there is a greater range in physical, mental, and moral characteristics among the Jews of New York than in any other people. After all, the Jewish element is recruited from very many lands, and out of each land the Jewish immigrant has taken on something of the color of the country. Some of the most abject poverty is found among the Jews, and also the greatest wealth. They are the spenders and hoarders. The Babbitts and the intellectuals. The aesthetes and the vulgarians. Indeed, they cover the entire range of human potentialities. There is no such person as "the Jew".

Professor Albert Einstein said in a speech before the Sorbonne:

> "If my theory of relativity is proven successful, Germany will claim me as a German and France will declare that I am a citizen of the world. Should my theory prove untrue, France will say that I am a German, and Germany will declare that I am a Jew."

* * *

Since we are dealing with a subject which is largely undocumented, it becomes necessary to consider a great deal of hearsay and casual conversational comment. For instance, in any intimate discussion between Jew and Gentile over the question of discrimination, the point will often be made, "But, after all, isn't it true that a great many Jews are personally unpleasant?" Here, of course, it is impossible to use any scientific formula. After all, who has a precise measuring rod for what is pleasant or unpleasant in other people? I think that this feeling of irritation against a certain number of Jews is a manifestation of the curious way in which a Gentile community attacks from both sides. Specifically, it is charged many Jews are pushing and aggressive, and yet in all logic it seems to me that this is the natural and inevitable result of applying pressure. When a man is discriminated against he will either sulk or rebel. Both modes of action may be identified in certain individual Jews.

It must be remembered that discrimination against Jews rests upon a pole precisely opposite to the prejudice against the Negro race. The so-called Nordic maintains that he cannot treat the Negro as an equal because he belongs to an inferior race. This charge is practically never raised against the Jew.

Whenever discrimination is justified by a self-conscious process of thought rather than taken on as a mere habit of mind, the charge runs that the Jew is too sharp, too successful, and even too arrogant. He has not endeared himself to the community by earning the title of the greatest money lender in the world. Today the greatest money lender is usually transferable into the greatest financier. Although connection with the house of Morgan or the Rockefeller family may be disadvantageous to any one seeking election, on the whole, people regard our moneyed kings with a certain warmth and admiration if they happen to be Gentiles, while there is resentment at the idea of vast holdings in the hands of any Jewish firm. This cannot be explained on the ground of any greater philanthropic element in the administration of Gentile fortunes. Everybody in New York knows that Jewish charities are probably the most wisely administered and effective of all group philanthropies. Even in periods of depression one seldom finds many Jews on the breadline or in the municipal lodging house.

I think that very probably irritation at the successful Jewish business man depends upon the basic anti-foreign feeling which has always been prevalent in America. In fact, it might as well be noted right now that Jewish prejudice is not essentially a religious prejudice. In other words, a Jew does not end all discrimination if he stands forward and says, "I am in no sense orthodox. I have no connection with any synagogue nor do I observe the religious holidays of my people, or care anything about such customs as the Mosaic dietary regulations." In fact, a special venom is sometimes reserved for a Jew who has cut away his roots from Judaism. The convert to Christianity is assailed with a certain number of jeers and jokes specially reserved for the renegade.

Here is another way in which the attack comes from both quarters, because prejudice in some cases is explained on the ground that the rigid customs of orthodoxy fit ill into the vast and complex makeup of a modern American city. Jewish prejudice may depend upon some such trivial factor as the irritation of a man who rushes out to get a suit of clothes pressed, only to find that his tailor is closed for the afternoon on account of a Jewish holiday which the Gentile customer had forgotten.

Again, we have the double standard of judgment in regard to names. There is the question that certain Jewish surnames seem odd and ridiculous to the American ear. I cite Wimpfheimer, Yawolinsky, Ginsberg. I don't mean that any of these names is, from a cosmic standpoint, funny. But simply, they have the nature of seeming strange and outlandish to a world of Browns, Smiths, and Blakes. It would seem, then, that everybody should be pleased when names, difficult to pronounce, and to certain ears ugly, are removed from circulation. We cry constantly that all who come to America should be assimilated and take on American manners and American customs. One of the first steps towards assimilation is to assume some other name which chimes in with the custom of the country. From that point of view a Mr. Yawolinsky who becomes Mr. Yale pays a tribute to the prejudices and manners of the community in which he lives. Yet, will he be applauded by any Jew-baiting Gentile? He will not. I have heard it said a hundred times that "Jews are tricky and are eager to change their names in order to pass as Gentiles." The problem is simply this: Any person with an obviously Jewish name is gravely handicapped in regard to obtaining many sorts of employment, while if he changes it he is viewed as one who has resorted to a subterfuge. In other words, this is one more case of "damned if you do and damned if you don't."

* * *

Prejudice seems to me more severe right now than at any time in the last twenty years. Of course, this is only an opinion. I speak from what I think I observe in New York life round about me. What has served to intensify the prejudice? It is hard to put your finger on any one thing. In case of doubt it is always wise to look for an economic cause. The business depression has tended to increase prejudice of all kinds. When jobs are hard to obtain, job-givers are anxious to disqualify some particular group of applicants, and as many applicants as possible. Specifically, of course, there is demand for stricter immigration laws to shut out the competition of the foreigner. Firms are asked to deny work to any but the native born when times are hard. The sex war is intensified, and the suggestion will frequently be made that men be employed instead of women, particularly in the case of married women, although the community is well aware that many married women are not working for pin money but for actual sustenance. Naturally, under conditions of hardship the job-seeker feels that he is better off if he holds a definite advantage over his Jewish competitors.

When times are booming, the average firm will ask in regard to a white-collar worker, "Is she a good stenographer, or a good bookkeeper, or a good file clerk?" But when it is possible to assemble three or four hundred applicants in response to a single want ad, then you will find the query—"What is your religion?" creeping into the employment questionnaire. Here, too, you will receive what purports to be a logical explanation for this condition. Large employers of labor, when they can be induced to talk of the question of discrimination, will say, "It is on account of the Jewish holidays. After all, ours is a highly geared organization, and it is disruptive to have employes taking additional time off. We have to give the Christian holidays in any case and the existence of Jewish holidays as well is an added burden".

I think that very seldom is this a truthful explanation. I discussed the matter with Rabbi Wise, who said: "A fair test can be made of the sincerity of this objection and it frequently has. I have known Jews to apply for jobs and make the definite stipulation that they would not ask for time off on Jewish holidays. But it never availed to give them a job in a concern committed to prejudice". I might add on my own that in a land palpably suffering from over-production, additional holidays might well be a blessing rather than a curse.

But I doubt if the economic cause is the sole reason for any increase in Jewish prejudice. At least, I believe I have run across another reason which might be semi-economic. With the growth of the Soviet Republic and Communist activity in New York, people have begun to see red as they did in regard to Socialists during the war and immediately afterwards. Many of the radical leaders in America have been Jewish. This is true of both the Communists and the Socialist Party. In the minds of many unthinking people radicalism is thought to be peculiarly a characteristic of the Jewish people. Under these circumstances the Jewish applicant is suspected of being a revolutionary who will disseminate propaganda in the store or shop, or even indulge in sabotage. Any cursory knowledge of Russian conditions will show that Soviet leadership has not been largely Jewish. But I am maintaining that prejudice exists for the most part in the minds of the uninformed.

In addition to everything else, Jews take on part of the ill-will which the rest of America feels for New York. New York has the largest Jewish population, and Jewish names are associated with the theatre, the motion picture industry, and the entertainment world in general. And so, Puritan prejudice will vent itself upon all and any who have a particular part in catering to the pleasure principle. In fact, this point was made in the now thoroughly discredited Protocols of Zion. These fake documents were used to foment the theory that Jewish theatrical managers and motion picture producers were consciously trying to impair the morals of the American people in order to make them weak and ripe for conquest.

Any newspaperman knows that a denial seldom has the same force as the original statement, and Mr. Henry Ford was not able to correct by his recantation the damage which he had done in furthering anti-Jewish prejudice. Unfortunately, the wild stories about the Protocols of Zion continue to circulate in back areas even after these forgeries are dead and gone. The vitality of an ancient myth is amazing. Not so many years ago in the Empire State of New York, a trooper made serious inquiries among the Jewish people of his neighborhood as to ritualistic murders, because a small child was missing.

* * *

Sooner or later in this discussion the question should be considered as to whether any book on the extent and nature of Jewish prejudice can serve a good purpose. I have long felt that I wanted to open the subject for discussion. A good many Jews have advised me to do no such thing. Their argument was that discrimination might be strengthened if attention was called to it. "Better let things slide along as they are" was the gist of this comment. I disagree. It seems to me that truth comes best out of full and free discussion. In fact, I work for a newspaper chain which carries on its editorial page the symbol of a lighthouse and the caption, "Give Light and the People will find their own way."

It must be admitted that the question of discrimination against Jews has been an undercover activity in America. Anti-semitism does not exist to any great extent here if you mean an official and open policy. There are no anti-semitic newspapers or magazines in the Metropolitan area. At one time *Life* carried on such a campaign, but that was abandoned years ago. Theoretically, there undoubtedly is prejudice which would flame into the open if a Jew ran for President. But even this has its limitations. It is worth noting that, with the exception of Governor Roosevelt, Herbert Lehman ran at the head of his ticket in the last gubernatorial election in which he was returned as Lieutenant-Governor.

Since the decline of the Klan I can think of no organization effective in the New York area which makes anti-semitism a part of its program. And yet it would be folly to deny the existence of the discrimination even though it has few, if any, open defenders. But there is one real risk in venturing into this field. The point was made by a Jewish friend of mine, who said, "If you point out that prejudice is common and widespread, you may serve to justify certain people in their conduct and in their opinions. They will say, 'If everybody else is doing it, why not I?' " However, the answer to this lies in the fact that the prejudice is by no means universal.

On page 49 of Norman Hapgood's book, *The Changing Years,* he describes a discussion which he had with President Eliot, of Harvard, regarding the selection of his successor:

> "He told me frankly why he did not favor the leading possibility, Mr. Lowell, and brought out his own choice, Mr. Jerome Green. I then presented the name of Mr. Louis D. Brandeis. Dr. Eliot was delighted. The question of social prejudice was far from giving him concern. Rather it added to his enthusiasm. On that part of the subject he said, 'I am a Unitarian. It would please me to be followed by a Jew. You know those seven men (the overseers) and what chance he will have, but I shall be pleased to put his name before them.' "

Dr. Eliot was a man of striking independence of thought, and yet he was essentially not only a New Englander but a Boston Brahmin. If Eliot could enthusiastically hail the possibility of a Jewish president of Harvard University, it must be evident that there are people in the community who would blow up utterly the whole matter of race prejudice.

* * *

In the beginning it seemed to me that we should confine ourselves largely to such discrimination as exists in regard to employment, education and housing. These are the really vital problems in anyone's life. I had planned to make little mention of such social discrimination as is exemplified in club membership, but the more I come to think of it, the more I am impressed that possible reforms in so-called trivial things may be the most important of all. Now and then, some successful member of the Jewish community will say in an interview that he has never encountered discrimination. Several of our most successful writers and journalists are Jewish—many of them extremely popular—and I think it is true that discrimination touches them very little. No manager would turn down a play because the author is Jewish. Magazine editors bid avidly for the fiction of Edna Ferber, and F. P. A. is probably as well liked as anybody now appearing in the daily newspapers. And yet, I feel that even in the case of these peculiarly gifted people, some stirring slight may lie in ambush. The minor rudeness, the inconsequential ban of some arrogant beach club, may cause terrific anguish to a sensitive soul. The prejudice of the college fraternity and the college club, can scar a youngster for his entire life.

Very probably, the best beginning in the abolition of prejudice would be the foundation of a true spirit of brotherhood; and this would mean a close social communion. It is well enough to say, "Oh, every club has a right to set whatever rules or traditions it pleases. If fifty men want to get together into a league of red hair, who can deny them permission to exclude all blondes and brunettes?" I think this reasoning isn't very sound.

I am also aware of the fact that there are Jewish fraternities and Jewish clubs which do not admit Gentiles. Later on, I think, I may develop the fact that a certain amount of discrimination and prejudice has been, if not precisely approved, at least accepted by many Jews. The brotherhood of which I am speaking is not wholly a one-sided arrangement. It must come from both camps.

My impression that social slights may be the most important of all was strengthened by a conversation that I had with a famous Jewish leader. I began by talking about employment, education, housing. He agreed that these were the considerations to be stressed. He spoke of several incidents within his own experience, and yet he tended to stray from the point. Again and again he brought up the fact that a certain New York club which supposedly is intended to afford a meeting place for college graduates, was shut tight against Jews. This seemed to be the ban which rankled most in his own heart, and I think it inevitably true that though sticks and stones can break no bones, straws can accomplish that destruction. The club tradition has always seemed to me the most baffling of discrimination.

In most cases a New York social club is a sort of big hotel where one goes to swim in the pool, to buy a pack of cigarettes on credit, or to cash a check. There are relationships ever so much more intimate. I am thinking of the case of a friend of mine who lived in Westchester. His friends and cronies were well-to-do and socially prominent Gentiles. He was Jewish. He went to their houses to dance and they came to his. Dinners were constantly being given by him and for him. And yet, when his name was put up for a New York club, controlled largely by his intimates, the barrier was drawn. Dancing and dining were one thing, and club membership quite another. And this barrier is one which can be raised so readily. Surely, the world would not crumble if every committee on admissions should suddenly wake up next Monday morning at nine o'clock and say, "Let's be done with this old nonsense." Indeed, I once sat in on what seemed to me the beginning of a break in the ice-jam. I was a member of a small organization made up of composers, journalists and actors. The man who ruled the club with imperial power showed me a list of men proposed for membership. One of them was a close newspaper friend of mine and I said, "If he wants to join I should think it would be fine for the club." The pooh-bah seemed embarrassed. "There wouldn't be any objections on the ground of his being Jewish, would there?" I asked. "I am afraid there would," said the club ruler. "But," I exclaimed in surprise, "we already have a number of Jewish members." I cited two composers, three violinists and one of the world's great pianists. "Oh, yes," said the club ruler, "musical Jews, but not any others." So possibly we can begin to found a new sort of society as soon as the whole world turns to song.

Chapter II

PETER STUYVESANT TO HENRY FORD

AMERICA owes its reputation as the land of promise for Jewish immigrants, perhaps, to the fact that it never tried to deal with its Jewish problem in the simple and effective way by which it solved the Indian problem. It seems never to have killed a Jew just because he was a Jew, as it has lynched the even less favored Negro because he was black. But the spirit of human hatred was one of the first settlers from across the Atlantic, and like the green bay tree it flourishes today. Prejudice on opposite shores of the ocean is very much the same, except in degree.

Notwithstanding the comparatively bright opportunities here and the freedom from pogroms, one can find in American history the duplicates of most of the types of prejudice against Jews which Europe affords. It is true that there are now almost no prizes or distinctions—short of being President of the United States—to which the superior individual Jew may not aspire as at least possible to him. But you may find in practical application a *numerus clausus* in colleges and professional schools. You may find the essence of the Ghetto spirit in the restriction of Jews from residence sections, apartments, and hotels. You may observe a boycott denying bread to Jews by shutting them out of jobs. Even where the hostility is invisible, it lurks often within what Dr. Joseph Jastrow calls "the subtle persecutions of neglect, exclusions, and disdain."

The most spectacular—and, one may add, scandalous and hilarious—outbreak of anti-Jewish prejudice in the United States probably was that which celebrated the funeral of Jacob Joseph, chief rabbi of the orthodox faith, one of the most revered and beloved of modern patriarchs. This leader of the largest congregation on the East Side of New York was gathered to his fathers on July 28, 1902. Two days later he was honored with the greatest funeral New York's Ghetto ever attended. A crowd of 50,000 persons followed the plain board coffin. From one synagogue to another it was drawn for repeated services of mourning on the way to the grave in Brooklyn.

Now it happened that the factory of R. Hoe & Co., manufacturers of printing presses, then at Grand and Sheriff Sts., directly in the route of the procession, employed a large number of pronounced antisemites who had been known among their Jewish neighbors for a long time as antagonistic, hostile and confirmed "whisker-pullers". The hearse reached the factory just at the time of the noon recess for lunch. As the close-packed column of Jews approached, it was greeted with jeers and yells of disrespect. The coffin was carried past. Then all of a sudden a bucket of water was thrown from an upper window upon the heads of the mourners. Next came "bundles of paper saturated with oil, bits of iron, small blocks of wood and other missiles." The mourners charged the building, hurled bricks, broke windows. The defenders turned on a fire hose. The police turned out on a riot call and aided the confusion by clubbing Jews over the head. It was a roaring shindy. It was perfectly gorgeous, perfectly melodramatic, perfectly savage. Ambulances treated about two dozen persons and it was estimated that more than one hundred others were injured.

Such a riot, one concedes, is but a trifle compared to the blood-stained tradition of the Old World, as illustrated for example in Somerset Maugham's story in *The Gentleman in the Parlour*. The scene is at the Peace Conference at Versailles:

> It appears that on one occasion M. Paderewski was pressing upon Mr. Wilson, Mr. Lloyd George and M. Clemenceau the Polish claims on Danzig.
>
> "If the Poles do not get it," he said, "I warn you that their disappointment will be so great there will be an outbreak, and they will assassinate the Jews."

> Mr. Wilson looked grave, Mr. Lloyd George shook his head, and M. Clemenceau frowned.
>
> "But what will happen if the Poles get Danzig?" asked Mr. Wilson.
>
> M. Paderewski brightened. He shook his leonine mane.
>
> "Ah, that will be quite another thing," he replied. "Their enthusiasm will be so great there will be an outbreak, and they will assassinate the Jews."

Humor such as this is rooted in long centuries of persecution. It traces to such things as the Crusaders on their way to the Holy Sepulchre pausing to slaughter Jewish communities, or to massacres of Jews for their supposed responsibility for the plague of the Black Death, or to the wholesale expulsions of Jews from one nation to another. It is based on a whole literature of hate, which might include such long ago writings as the legend of Hugh of Lincoln, murdered by the Jews, and Chaucer's *Prioress's Tale,* and Martin Luther's treatise on *The Jews and Their Lies.* And, of course, the unrelieved old Ghetto is in the background, the cramped slum in which the despised exotic race was confined in its misery.

Antagonism toward Jews in America has been, at various times, religious, political, economic, social, or combinations of these and other types. The colony of Maryland was exceedingly tolerant in its early days toward all kinds of Christian dissenters, but its laws provided death for any person who denied the Trinity. However, there is no record of a Jew having been executed. All the traditional insults uttered against the Jews by that classical Roman anti-semite, Apion, have been repeated in America, except the item that they were descendants of lepers. Today one of the strong bases of prejudice probably is a feeling of social superiority; the feeling that these people are newcomers with ways that are different, a race that appeared often either as peddlers or as sewers-on of buttons, who were seen only a few years ago coming in from Ellis Island with shawls on their heads instead of hats, and misshapen bundles instead of chic luggage, who clutter up the subways now and eat *gefuellte fisch* in the parks on hot Sunday afternoons.

Jews are not the only sufferers from prejudice, to be sure. Negroes are much worse off. The Irish and Italians have carried similar handicaps. All foreigners share the Jewish experience in part. And prejudice is not accepted by all Jews as a tragedy. Many thrive on it, and others joke about it. The late Rabbi Maurice H. Harris remarked, "Darwin taught the doctrine of the survival of the fittest. I will not say that we Jews are the fittest, but we certainly have survived."

New York is the great seat of Jews in America, and the stronghold of prejudice. Everywhere one hears, "New York would be all right if it were not for the damned Jews." Prejudice is explained as the result of the great number of Jews and their sharp competition with Gentiles for money, space, even for air to breathe. There are just too many Jews, it seems; and there always have been. In the first chapter of the second book of the Bible, Pharaoh of Egypt tells his people, "Behold, the people of the Children of Israel are more and mightier than we." Therefore, they did set over them taskmasters to afflict them with their burdens. In Palestine just now the Arabs insist there are too many Jews. Whatever the number, there are persons to call it too many.

When there was only one Jew in America, he was too many and was rejected. His name was Solomon Franco, mentioned in the records of the Massachusetts Bay Colony on May 3, 1649, and he was about to be sent back to Holland. The court kindly granted him six shillings a week for ten weeks as subsistence until he could get passage on a ship.

Peter Stuyvesant did not want the Jews when they first sought refuge in New Amsterdam. The colonial period was one long struggle for emancipation; the republic again and again has produced outbursts of prejudice; and since the War there have been the two tremendous influences of hatred represented by the Klu Klux Klan and the *Dearborn Independent.* Jewish immigrants have leaped to surprising wealth and eminence, and the story of the Jews in America is one of heroic and successful accomplishment. But its details remain a constant record of doors slammed in the face, hurdles raised in the path, and shoulders contemptuously turned away.

* * *

The American story of Jewish persecution dates to the initial year of 1492. Columbus wrote that "after the Spanish monarchs had expelled all the Jews from all their kingdoms and lands in April, in the same month they commissioned me to undertake the voyage to India." While the discoverer was away on that voyage, Ferdinand and Isabella confiscated for the state treasury all property which had belonged to Jews. This spoil financed the admiral's second voyage in 1463.

The first settlement of Jews in America seems to have been at New Amsterdam in 1654, ten years before the colony was captured by the British, and twenty-eight years after Manhattan Island was bought from the Indians.

On August 22, 1654, a lone Jew, Jacob Barsimson or Barsimon, arrived from Holland on the ship *Pereboom,* and a few weeks later a party of twenty-three came on board the *St. Charles,* having been driven out of Brazil. They were given temporary shelter but not a welcome. Governor Stuyvesant asked them to get out. He reported this to the directors of the Dutch West India Company in Amsterdam, begging support for his policy, "that the deceitful race—such hateful enemies and blasphemers of the name of Christ—be not allowed further to infect and trouble this new colony to the detraction of your worships and the dissatisfaction of your worships' most affectionate subjects."

The directors replied rather apologetically, but on the side of liberality, telling Stuyvesant "that these people may travel and trade to and in New Netherlands and remain there, provided the poor among them shall not become a burden to the company or to the community, but be supported by their own nation. You will now govern yourself accordingly." In the same letter the directors admitted that "we foresee the same difficulties which you fear." However, the Jews had nowhere else to go and exclusion might be "unreasonable and unfair;" furthermore, the Jews were to be admitted "also because of the large amount of capital which they still have invested in the shares of this company."

For a year or two Stuyvesant grumbled about having the Jews on his hands, and the directors insisted upon his treating them generously. At the governor's elbow was the fussing Dominie Megapolensis, saying that his congregation resented the aliens because they had no other God than "the unrighteous Mammon" and no other aim than "to get possession of Christian property." However, the dominie's church spent several hundred guilders in relieving the want of the newcomers.

The governor wrote, October 30, 1655, that "to give liberty to the Jews would be very detrimental because the Christians there will not be able at the same time to do business. Giving them liberty, we cannot refuse the Lutherans and Papists." June 10, 1656, he wrote, "with regard to trade they are not hindered, but trade with the same privileges and freedom as other inhabitants. Also they have many times requested of us the free and public exercise of their abominable religion, but this cannot yet be accorded them." In exasperation at the directors' leniency, he added, "What they may be able to obtain from your honors, time will tell."

The directors wrote to Stuyvesant on March 13, 1656, that "the permission given to the Jews to go to New Netherlands and enjoy the same privileges as they have here (in Amsterdam) has been granted only as far as civil and political rights are concerned, without giving the said Jews a claim to the privileges of exercising their religion in a synagogue or at a gathering." However, this did not forbid the Jewish religion "in all quietness within their own houses." In a letter dated June 14, 1656, the directors reprimanded Stuyvesant for discrimination and directed obedience "punctually and with more respect."

Jewish settlements, at the same time, were being

established up and down the Atlantic Coast. The next earliest was in Rhode Island, Roger Williams' religious free state. The first group of fifteen families arrived in Newport in 1658, and they, according to legend, first introduced Freemasonry into the United States. However, they were not accepted with any warmth, merely promised "as good protection as any stranger being not of our nation residing among us in His Majesty's colony ought to have, being obedient to His Majesty's laws." This declaration was made by the legislature in 1684.

The English governor of New York, Burnet, announced a notable advance in liberalism in his order of November 15, 1727, permitting Jews in taking oath in court to omit the phrase, "upon the true faith of a Christian."

Race prejudice could be invoked for the sake of politics in those days just as practically as it is today. The great outburst came in an election contest in September, 1737. Colonel Adolph Philipse, on the aristocratic ticket, was running for representative in the General Assembly against Cornelius Van Horne, the democrat. Both sides were active in getting out the vote. "The sick, the blind, the lame, Jews, soldiers from the garrisons, many who had been bedridden, men from prison and poorhouse were brought in carriages to the place of election." There was fighting and quarreling. The quotation is from Phelps Stokes' *Iconography.*

Philipse won by a count of 413 to 399. But Van Horne's friends protested and retained Attorney William Smith, the firebrand orator. Most of the Jewish votes had been cast for Philipse, and Smith objected, not only to the testimony of Jews being heard, but to their votes being counted. He made a great speech, appealing to the religious prejudices and passions of the assembly, reading, from a Bible in his hand, of the sufferings of Jesus Christ, "and so affected his audience that the house resolved that the Jews not having the right to vote for members of Parliament, could not for representative." Ironically, Philipse retained his seat anyhow, for his attorneys caused a large number of Van Horne's votes likewise to be thrown out.

Three years later the British Parliament provided for the naturalization of Jews in the colonies, and thirty-five Jews were admitted in New York. The poll lists show them voting later in the colonial period.

And so the record of the Jews in the American colonies may be brought to a placid ending with the following surprised observation in 1748 by Peter Kalm, the Swedish botanist:

"There are many Jews settled in New York who possess great privileges. They have a synagogue and houses, great country seats of their own property and are allowed to keep shops in the town. They have likewise several ships which they freight and send out with their goods; in fine, the Jews enjoy all the privileges in common with the other inhabitants of this town and province."

* * *

The Declaration of Independence and the Constitution put an end, theoretically, to racial discrimination. There were only two thousand Jews in the country at the time of the Revolution, and the outstanding one was Haym Salomon from Poland. He contributed a great part of his fortune to finance the war. Washington, Jefferson and other political leaders were outspoken in friendship to the Jews.

A Jew became governor of Georgia in March, 1801, the first of his race to achieve this particular type of distinction. He was David Emanuel, sixth governor of Georgia, for whom also a county in the state has been named. The pessimist concerning prejudice may find a talking point in the fact that Governor Emanuel seems not to have been a very Jewish Jew, there being an unconfirmed report that he had become a member of the Presbyterian church. His daughters and sisters married Christians.

Following the early immigration of the Spanish and Portuguese Jews, the *Sephardim,* there came in the forties and fifties of the nineteenth century a tide of German Jews, the *Ashkanazim,* fleeing political persecution as revolutionists. Either coincidentally or logically, there arose now the first real American organization of race and religious prejudice. It was the Know Nothing Party. Its main blasts were against Roman Catholicism, but the Jews caught the backwash.

During the Civil War there were anti-Jewish slurs in the North because of the prominence of Judah P. Benjamin in the Confederacy. And both General Grant and General Ben F. Butler openly expressed anti-Jewish feeling, for which both publicly apologized. The Grant incident centered around his famous Order No. 11, inspired by reports of Jewish traders running the blockade and buying Southern cotton. The order, dated Holly Springs, December 17, 1862, said:

> The Jews, as a class violating every regulation of trade established by the Treasury Department and also department orders, are hereby expelled from the Department within twenty-four hours from the receipt of this order.
>
> Post commanders will see that all of this class of people be furnished passes and required to leave, and any one returning after such notification will be arrested and held in confinement until an opportunity occurs of sending them out as prisoners, un-

> less furnished with permit from headquarters.
>
> No passes will be given these people to visit headquarters for the purpose of making personal applications for trade permits.
>
> By order of Major General Grant.
>
> John A. Rawlins, Asst. Adjutant General.

Grant had been harboring this feeling for some time. On November 10, he had written one of his generals, "Give orders to all the conductors on the road that no Jews are to be permitted to travel on the railroad southward from any point. They may go north and be encouraged in it, but they are such an intolerable nuisance that the department must be purged of them."

Order No. 11 was short-lived, however. On January 4, 1863, General Halleck, the general-in-chief in Washington, sent Grant this curt message:

> "A paper purporting to be general order No. 11 issued by you December 17 has been presented here. By its terms it expels all Jews from your department. If such an order has been issued, it will be immediately revoked."

This slip of Grant's was to arise later to plague

him as a candidate for the presidency. In the heat of the campaign, September 14, 1868, he wrote an explanation to Congressman I. N. Morris of Illinois, saying, "The letter was issued and sent without any reflection and without thinking of the Jews as a sect or race to themselves, but simply as persons who had violated an order, which greatly inured to the help of the rebels. Give Mr. Moses assurance that I have no prejudice against sect or race, but want each individual to be judged by his own merit."

Now long before this time the original *Sephardim* had reached positions of wealth and aristocratic exclusiveness, and by the 1880's the later German Jews were getting a foothold, financially and socially. The Jewish race in America numbered about two hundred and thirty thousand. Then, on March 13, 1881, in Russia, occurred an event of the most vital personal importance to every Jew in America. An anarchist tossed a bomb into the lap of the liberal Tsar Alexander II in St. Petersburg. Provoked by his father's assassination, Alexander III, the new Tsar, began a series of extreme retaliatory and reactionary policies, and he took his spite out particularly on the Jews. They had the choice between apostacy, starvation, or emigration. The terrorized stampede of Russian, Polish, and Roumanian Jews to get away from pogroms and persecutions found its principal spillway into the United States. The word Jew in this country, by the very forces of numbers, became identified with these new arrivals, a distressed, lowly, alien mass in the lower East Side of New York, heedlessly eager to seize the opportunities of the land of promise.

This immigration from Eastern Europe brought more than 2,000,000 Jews into the United States within thirty years. The Jewish Communal Survey has carried its estimates down to the year 1928 and placed the Jewish population of New York then at 1,835,000. It predicted that by 1933 it would reach 2,000,000. The figure is nearly one-third the city's total. The Jewish population of the United States was estimated at 4,228,000, or more than one-fourth of all the Jews in the world. Long before this total was reached, the cry was raised against "too many Jews."

The torrent of Jewish immigrants received an arbitrary check from the temporary Immigration Act of 1921, and the policy of restriction was made permanent by the "national origins" quota law of 1924. Cutting down the intake from Russia, Poland and Eastern Europe, the law produced the effect of diminishing Jewish immigration to an average of 10,972 or 4.88 percent of the annual total. Jewish immigration in 1914 had reached a peak of 138,051, and during the five years preceding 1924 it had averaged 57,312 or 10.4 percent of the total. Jewish leaders fought the enactment of the 1924 law and still resent it as practical discrimination against their race.

Anti-semitism as a way of thinking and of political action—as distinguished from religious prejudice—was revived in Europe at about the same time the Russian migration started across the Atlantic. Missionaries of anti-semitism swiftly pursued the Russians to America. Among the first of these was the German, Herrmann Ahlwardt, who arrived in 1896 to preach the doctrine in New York.

Theodore Roosevelt, then police commissioner, with his eye for drama, politics, and the larger gesture, turned Ahlwardt into a joke by assigning Jewish policemen exclusively to guard him and protect him from interference.

* * *

Hate against Jews in the United States has been fanned since the War as never before. The most serious campaigns ever waged in America probably have been those of the Ku Klux Klan and of Henry Ford. At the same time that Ford was publishing in his *Dearborn Independent* the "Protocols of the Wise Men of Zion," exposing the alleged plans for the Jewish domination of the world, there were printed also Burton J. Hendrick's hostile volume, *The Jews in America,* and the English anonymous attack, *The Cause of World Unrest.*

Although the Klan's power is broken and its prominence is in eclipse, occasional incidents still reveal its presence. Such survivals may be only freaks. But if the organization has been dissipated, the spirit persists. In the spring of 1930, within ten miles of New York City, there occurred a verified example of Klan influence. A suburban village approached an election for police justice in which the only candidates were three Catholics and a Jew. The Klan organization held a meeting to decide upon a choice in this dilemma. It was agreed, after long discussion, that undesirable as was any Jew, a Catholic would be worse. This word was passed around by the Klan, as an organization in its own name. When the votes were counted, the Jew had won by about twelve hundred out of a total vote of two thousand.

Calm and well-informed Jews today, in discussing Henry Ford's propaganda of opposition, give him credit, whether he wills it now or not, as the greatest of all factors in stirring up an increased and widespread antagonism. His campaign began in 1920 and continued until his open letter of retraction and apology dated June 30, 1927, addressed to Louis Marshall, president of the American Jewish Committee. Ford's dislike of Jews arose, according to the Reverend Dr. Charles F. Aked, one of his companions on the peace ship, because he blamed Madame Rosika Schwimmer, a Jewess, as the "evil genius" of the expedition. Ford himself said he conceived the idea for his anti-Jewish campaign on that trip, getting an "insight into the responsibility for the war and who profited by it." After seven years of vilification, he ceased abruptly, announcing:—

> "I confess that I am deeply mortified that this journal which is intended to be constructive and not destructive has been made the medium for resurrecting exploded fictions, for giving currency to the so-called 'Protocols of the Wise Men of Zion,' which have been demonstrated, as I learn, to be gross forgeries, and for contending that the Jews have been engaged in a conspiracy to control the capital and the industries of the world, besides laying at their door many offenses against decency, public order and good morals."

He said also:

> "I frankly confess that I have been greatly shocked as a result of my study and examination of the files of the *Dearborn Independent* and of the pamphlets entitled *The International Jew.* I deem it to be my duty as an honorable man to make amends for the wrong done to the Jews as fellow-men and brothers, by asking their forgiveness for the harm that I have unintentionally committed, by retracting so far

> as lies within my power the offensive charges laid at their door by these publications, and by giving them the unqualified assurance that henceforth they may look to me for friendship and good will."

Since that announcement, active propaganda against Jews in America may be called almost nonexistent. A certain amount is found among Russian emigres, preserving the imperial tradition of anti-semitism. From such sources, supposedly, spring most of the defamatory handbills and cartoons which are passed around by hand in foreign-speaking districts.

In its way the Leo M. Frank case at Atlanta, Georgia, culminating in Frank's lynching in August, 1915, was a unique tragedy in Jewish annals. It was called the American Dreyfus case. The fact that Frank was a Jew, however, was but one element. A more recent incident which brought a momentary flare-up of indignation among Jews far and wide was the revival of the old human sacrifice slander at the village of Massena, N. Y., in September, 1928. A four-year-old child was lost on the eve of Yom Kippur, and the mayor sent a state trooper to inquire of the rabbi if it were true that Jews customarily celebrated the holdiday with the shedding of blood. Later the child was found, unharmed. In response to a memorable protest, both mayor and trooper apologized and the latter was suspended "for gross lack of discretion and conduct unbecoming an officer."

Petty expressions of prejudice, naturally, are of every day occurrence. There are threats of legislation to make more rigid the observance of Sunday as a day of rest, to the detriment of Jewish Sabbath observers, and there is agitation for compulsory Bible-reading in public schools. Occasionally a performance of the Passion Play or the showing of a film such as *The King of Kings* is protested as sowing seeds of prejudice. On the other hand, Jews, Catholics, and Protestants are meeting together more and more in conferences for the express purpose of better understanding, and there are many instances of congregational brotherliness such as the Temple Beth-El in New York inviting the Reverend Dr. Harry Emerson Fosdick and his Baptist following to worship on Sundays in the temple, while the new Riverside Church was under construction.

The Federal Council of the Church of Christ in America has created a committee on good will. Its secretary, the Reverend Everett R. Clinchy, writing recently in *The Christian Century* of frictions which he was seeking to erase, mentioned these current incidents:

> "A community in Delaware has met in a Baptist Church over a period of years,

observing Thanksgiving Day. The Jews have attended in admirable numbers and two rabbis have taken part. Last November one of the participating clergymen prayed 'for this fellowship of Christian churches,' but never once recognized the loyal Jews. Of course, this was thoughtlessness, for afterward he could not remember that he prayed for any fellowship. . .

"In Texas three ministers left the platform of a joint meeting because a rabbi was to speak; they would not listen! . . . In Louisiana a minister refused to meet with a joint committee to consider community cooperation, saying that he 'would not sit at a table with one who denied my Lord.' In Illinois a Protestant minister announced a Sunday evening community mass meeting for everybody; his subject was, 'The Problem of the Jew, or How Shall We Get Rid of Him?' "

Such a long parading of evidence to prove the existence of prejudice, of course, is unnecessary. The point is conceded or, more often, proclaimed. Looking at the exhibit, however, one must be impressed by the almost unchanging attitude of the prejudiced heart in spite of "civilization"; so that the American view toward alien customs and blood coincides remarkably with that of the Medes and Persians at the time of Esther in the Bible, when Haman said unto King Ahasuerus:

> "There is a certain people scattered abroad and dispersed among the people in all the provinces of thy kingdom; and their laws are diverse from all people; neither keep they the king's laws; therefore it is not for the king's profit to suffer them."

Chapter III

"SOME OF MY BEST—"

A CURIOUS factor in Jewish and Gentile relations is the so-called pet Jew. He is the person referred to in the very familiar phrase "some of my best friends are Jews." In arguing that the community in general does not consciously approve of discrimination, one need only refer to this almost inevitable remark which is made by Gentiles in general when they feel that they are under any reproach or accusation of prejudice. Of course, it is no answer at all. Many a man who blithely and proudly says, "Many of my best friends are Jews," is also an employer who does draw religious lines in his office; or he may be connected with a school or college which imposes a quota system.

To be sure, some part of a new freedom might be distilled from the old stock phrase. The Babbitt who says, "Some of my best friends are Jews," is giving testimony against the old belief in a set type of person called "the Jew". Once you admit the possibility and, indeed, the existence of exceptions, any general rule of discrimination should break down. Not even the most ardent champion against discrimination would care to maintain that unpleasant and disagreeable Jews do not exist. He merely argues that any rule of conduct should be based on the individual, and not the group.

The British often say the same things against Americans that Gentile Americans say against the Jews.

The British say that Americans are loud, vulgar, disrespectful, unsporting, ostentatious with their money, dishonest, superficial in learning, greedy, materialistic, pushing, a bad influence on the fine old traditions of the Anglo-Saxon race, that they swarm across the ocean every summer and spoil the real Old England, that their children are impossible, and that, whereas the individual may be all right, the mass of them is atrocious.

There is hardly a single charge against the Jews which the complacent and prejudiced Gentile American makes which is not made against the American by the European, particularly by the Britisher.

The American tourist who has been embarrassed by loud fellow-Americans abroad will concede most of these points. But whenever he, himself, is not recognized as an acceptable individual, whenever he is rebuffed because he is classed with those terrible Americans, he feels a great indignation. He realizes that the foreign attitude is pure benighted prejudice.

One of the most bitterly critical and perhaps prejudiced books against the United States was C. E.

M. Joad's *The Babbitt Warren,* published in 1926. After a sweeping attack the author reaches the following conclusion:

> "There are Americans who are gentle, courteous and tolerant, men of knowledge and understanding, capable of fine shades of feeling and a sensitive consideration for the feelings of others, and possessing a culture all their own. We all know such Americans and value them the more for the contrast they present to their more prominent fellow countrymen."

Substitute the word Jews for Americans, and you express perfectly the attitude of, "Why, some of my best friends—"

* * *

Practically all the familiar charges held against this mythical person, the Jew, seem to me unsound. To a large extent they are built around a figure which used to appear frequently in the joke papers and in burlesque shows and slapstick comedy of one sort or another. For instance, you will find people who profess to believe that members of the Jewish race are extraordinarily avaricious and extremely stingy in money matters. While I cannot profess to have taken a census of miserliness among the millions, within my own experience this charge is very far from the facts. Indeed, I may point out that it is generally admitted by department store heads, theatrical producers, and restaurant men, that Jews are among the most lavish spenders in New York City. A certain recklessness with money would seem to me more characteristic than the hoarding principle. Nor was it ever particularly logical for a Gentile to say, "I can't get along with Jews because they squeeze their money so hard," since in our own day a counter-legend has arisen. There is an entire school of humor made up of Scotch jokes. The myth of the careful Scot may be legendary, but at least it has entered into the popular mind. Yet this far-flung conception of the close-fisted Highlander has not been reflected in any form of discrimination against the Scot.

I have already mentioned that other familiar charge that the Jew is loud, aggressive and pushing. Here again we come upon the familiar habit of confusing the group and the individual. For instance, if a Gentile is dining in a restaurant and observes across the room a Jewish patron who is making a good deal of noise, quarreling with the waiter, ordering an elaborate supper in an ostentatious way, he is almost certain to say, "Look at that vulgar Jew over there." But the same sort of conduct upon the part of a non-Jew will pass unnoticed, or, if it does attract attention, the offending individual would be merely stigmatized by "Look at that vulgar man."

There will be no attempt to classify him as French, English, High Church or Low. He errs upon his own. This fact came sharply to my notice once at a concert in Carnegie Hall where one of the great violinists of the world was playing. A couple were whispering and chattering during the performance and as we went out a friend of mine began to harangue me on the bad manners of Jews and their lack of musical appreciation. He assumed, whether correctly or not, that the offenders were Jewish. I met the argument by saying, "But, after all, there wouldn't even have been a concert without Jewish musical appreciation," for the artist of the occasion was Jascha Heifetz.

To get back to some of the damage done by what we may call the pet Jew procedure. While it may serve as an argument for individual consideration of individual cases, it does buoy up a certain smug acceptance of things as they are. I am referring particularly to the fact that certain favored Jews will chime in with Gentile prejudice. I mean, if some particular well-known Jewish family sends a son or daughter to what we call an "exclusive" school, that same family won't worry about the fact that the school has a quota system, or even a semi iron-clad rule against the admission of any Jews whatsoever. I have talked with three or four well-known Jewish business men on the question of the attitude of many colleges in regard to Jewish barriers, and often I have been surprised, and I may say, shocked, to find my Jewish acquaintances saying, "Well, there's much to be said for that policy." This is the remark of a man who feels that the policy has not or will not handicap his own son, so what does he care about the rest?

With the exception of a few stalwart and fiery leaders the Jewish community in New York does little to fight many frequent forms of discrimination. One could shout from the housetops that some department store or other refuses to employ Jews in its sales force. That would not mean, in all probability, that the Jewish buying public would immediately say, "Well, we will go elsewhere and not trade at that establishment." Certainly, even the most severe sort of exclusion practiced in several colleges has not led to a boycott upon the part of those against whom the discrimination was levelled. Here, of course, one might argue from the Jewish standpoint that if the college presents exceptional educational advantages the young Jew will fight to gain admission even though he knows that a definite quota system is employed. Discrimination in college goes deeper than the official attitude of the faculty. I have always held that part of student prejudice might be traced to professorial or presidential policy. But I grant that even in the most liberally administered institution students could kick up rows under their own steam.

The fraternity system bears harshly upon the Jewish undergraduate. The foundation of Jewish fraternities is of tolerably recent growth. In a way, it serves as an effective answer to the familiar practice of the old Greek letter societies in barring Jews. But it does set up a dangerous duality of existence. If there are to be Gentile fraternities and Jewish fraternities, it might be also logical to have within the same institution a Gentile baseball team and a Jewish baseball team, and to carry this division through all college activities. Of late there has been a good deal of talk of founding in America a Jewish university. I am afraid this would be an admission, almost an acceptance, of discrimination. No man who thinks closely on the question should care to commit himself to an America in which sharp religious lines are to be drawn in all walks of life.

Very often a college fraternity will select a young Jewish student for membership. Every college has this same story and it follows identical lines. The boy in most cases says when chosen, "Would it have made any difference if you knew that I was Jewish?" Thereupon there is a scurrying of the members back to the Chapter House. The boys go into a huddle and decide that it was courageous and frank on the part of the student to declare his religious affiliation in spite of the fact that it might tend to bar him. And in most cases, under the stress of a nascent liberalism, the Jewish boy becomes a brother, and I might add, a pet Jew.

I have argued that the proper conduct for the Jewish student in such cases is to refuse membership. He knows that he is going into an organization where his particular membership will merely constitute an exception to the rule. But I grant that there is room for debate. Several of my Jewish friends have argued that the lone member becomes, whether socially or not, a missionary and a propagandist for tolerance; that if he turns out to be a likeable and popular member of the group certain old delusions will go down. The same thing has happened in certain New York clubs. Yet, I stick to my contention that universal tolerance can come best by a certain solidarity upon the part of the Jewish community. I feel that if resentment were more articulate, many practices of discrimination could be broken down.

* * *

In support of this I will point to what happened at Harvard. President Lowell announced, about eight years ago, that Harvard was giving serious consideration to the question of limiting the number of Jews in the university. He brought up arguments in favor of this proposition which have since become extremely familiar. There was the one about the university's desire to represent a cross-section of the community. He also spoke of the fact that very many Jewish students in Harvard lived at home and merely came to attend lectures without actually entering into the life of the university. And during a subsequent discussion over the proposed quota system, Dr. Lowell made the statement that it was necessary to restrict Jewish enrollment because he found that the moral influence of students from this group was open to question. As proof, he cited that out of all the thefts of books from the Widener Library, those which had been traced to definite culprits showed that the Jews were one hundred percent guilty. The statement was checked and found to be absolutely true. One hundred percent of the discovered thieves were Jewish. But that one hundred percent consisted of just one man! No other case of theft had been traced. President Lowell used the familiar practice of generalizing upon a single example.

In the case of Harvard there was a very vigorous and concerted protest against the proposed policy of instituting the quota system. Many prominent Jews got into the fight as well as a number of distinguished Gentiles. Indeed, comment was so hot that President Lowell dropped the scheme and there is no quota system at Harvard today, not even a secret one.

In justice to President Lowell, it is only fair to say that he brought into the open a policy which was not only considered, but adopted, by a large number of universities. The manner in which discrimination is carried on in secret will be discussed in a later chapter.

Any testimony which I give about Harvard will concern the university of twenty years ago. In spite of the dispute centering around President Lowell's statement and a more recent controversy concerning the fact that divisional examinations were held on Yom Kippur, I still believe that Harvard is one of the institutions where the Jewish student suffers least from discrimination. Possibly this is more or less generally true of the big college as opposed to the little one, particularly if that big college is situated in a city. For instance, it is not of absolutely vital moment whether one belongs to a club in Harvard or not. Beyond the borders of the college one has access to the cultural activities of Boston and may readily spend a more pleasant evening at a symphony concert than lolling about the fraternity house. On the other hand, my experience has been that at Cornell or Dartmouth or Williams, where the college overshadows the town, the student is badly off if he happens to be a non-fraternity man. This applies to the Gentile barbarian as well as to the Jewish one.

The fraternity idea, as I see it, depends upon a selective process. The fun of joining consists of the fact that somebody else is not taken in. Rarely does the percentage of fraternity membership go over three-fifths of the total enrollment, and I imagine that the Jewish fraternities are likely to follow the pattern set by the Gentiles and elevate a certain number in their own community at the expense of others.

The question of anti-semitism in college is a difficult one because so much is not a matter of precise record or ascertainable incident, but merely details of conduct; and here, undeniably, imagination enters in. The Jewish student who is not particularly popular with his fellows is very likely to set up a defense mechanism and say, "This was done to me," or, "That was left undone because I am Jewish." Now, this could be the case, but it might also happen that the individual in question will not appeal wholly aside from his racial or religious connections. George Kaufman, the playwright, once outlined a tragic plot of a comedy which is not yet written. It concerned a man afflicted by a dread malady much popularized in flamboyant advertising. Even his best friends wouldn't tell him. In time he discovered a mouth wash which was to remove all barriers. He used it. He was cured. And found that even so people didn't like him.

In my time at Harvard there were clubs which rigorously excluded Jewish students, but this was not by any means a one hundred percent practice. I belonged to a fraternity which has since become a local club, and in the years from 1906 to 1910 about one-tenth of the membership was Jewish. I cannot remember that the point ever came up in discussion. We were not in any sense self-consciously tolerant. And yet I imagine that it was a little more difficult to obtain the election of a Jewish student. He had to be rather more desirable than any potential Gentile competitor.

The charge sometimes made that discrimination is exercised against Jews even in the matter of forming athletic teams doesn't seem to hold good at Harvard. There have been numerous prominent Jewish football and baseball players. I may cite the fact that Isidor Zarakov was captain of the baseball team; and for the last five years the football squad has been coached by a Jewish alumnus, Arnold Horween. Any statistical survey would show a comparatively small proportion of Jewish letter men. but this, I think, may be explained on the ground that the average Jewish student is less apt to be proficient or interested in college sports. For one thing, he is less likely to have been graduated from any one of the big preparatory schools where competition is fostered. The tradition behind him impels him to scholarship rather than athletics. Indeed, part of college prejudice against the Jewish student rests upon the fact that he is more passionate for Phi Beta Kappa than for the football team. In many cases the Jewish student goes to college under grave economic handicaps. Of course, a certain number of Gentiles work their way through, but it is more rare for the Gentile family in poor circumstances to make the sacrifices necessary for higher education. In the College of the City of New York, for instance, there are numberless Jewish boys who have to carry on an outside job not only sufficient to render them self-supporting, but also to enable them to contribute to the family's support. The avid hunger for learning is far more characteristic of the young Jew than of the young Gentile, and curiously enough, this is often used as a reproach. The phrase "greasy Jew grind" is all too common.

At Harvard failure to participate in any major sport was no reproach twenty years ago. In fact, the university prided itself that on the day of the Yale game the chess team might be meeting in fierce rivalry, or the Greek Club holding a conference. It was in the days of President Eliot a go-as-you-please university, both as to athletics and education. Much of this, I fear, has been changed. Class-consciousness has been introduced by the innovation of the freshman dormitory, and President Lowell has frankly worked to promote a group atmosphere something like that existing at Oxford and Cambridge. Social contacts are becoming, to some extent, compulsory, and it may be that in this forced companionship the Jewish student suffers from some degree of discrimination.

The Harvard of today, according to recent figures, consists of approximately 8,000 students, with 2,000 more in the woman's college, Radcliffe. Rabbi

Leon Spitz, in a detailed study, estimated the Jewish population at 1,000 men and women, or about eleven per cent. Here are his figures as to the various departments:

The College, 9 to 10 per cent; the Law School, 15 per cent; the School of Commerce, nearly 20 per cent; Medical, 8 per cent; Radcliffe, 12 per cent, in proportion to the non-Jews.

I have a letter from a student now at Harvard. He begins with a discussion of the club system, and writes in answer to our inquiry:

> "Harvard has a club system comparable to those at Yale and Princeton. Because I am not a member of any of them I cannot say from knowledge that they do not admit Jews, but I can say that out of about 30-40 clubs at Harvard, Jews are *seldom* if ever elected and only then, when they have constantly associated with Gentiles from their freshman year, have wealth, and more than likely come from fashionable prep schools which are recognized at Harvard.
>
> "You put it very broadly when you say 'quota restrictions.' (The restriction can't even be called a quota, but after all why are they not justified?) To conclude this answer, as I see I am getting away from

what you want, I will definitely say that from their actions as regards taking in new members, practically all of the more important and better clubs at Harvard do not ever take in Jewish boys. (Though some break their necks, pocketbooks and self respect trying to break in).

"I am speaking primarily of the social clubs. However, there is at Harvard an institution called the Institute of 1776, a social club, which has a wide membership, and is supposed to include all men who have some social, athletic, or personality distinction. This club has elected several Jewish boys to membership within the last few years, such as Al Miller, Izzy Zarakov, Lou Gordon, F. M. Warburg and perhaps one or two others. The active roll of the club is about one hundred and fifty or so, so you can see the proportion. But why should we complain—we don't invite Gentiles to our fraternities—even though they probably wouldn't accept.

"I really can't tell you the quota proportions, as theoretically there aren't any such things, but I do say that there are some clubs from which, by virtue of being a Jew, a Jew is automatically excluded, as exemplified by the fact that NO Jews are members, for example, the Porcellian Club.

"As far as I know I would say that Jews are eligible for the honorary societies, though I really don't know of many at Harvard except Phi Beta Kappa and Tau Beta Pi, both honorary, and to which Jews are elected. There is a Harvard Dramatic Club, which, out of a roster of sixty or so, has about five Jewish members. (I don't believe in going into distinctions between the supposed-to-be different kinds of Jews, but the supposedly better Jews are here elected, though the several boys I know who are members are good Jews, whereas some of the others to my opinion might as well be Gentiles, for it seems to me that is what they are trying to be).

"And now as I think about it some more, it comes to me that the early training of the boy, whether it be reform, conservative or orthodox, has a lot to do with his later behavior on the campus, but it really is a pity to see how there is an ascending line of vision among many, a false and artificial one. There may be some honorary societies from which the Jewish boy is excluded, but I am not sure.

"Well, there is the Harvard *Lampoon,*

Crimson, and *Advocate.* I have yet to see a real Jewish name on the boards of any of these publications. A "Cohen" has as much chance to be the editor of Harvard *Crimson* as I have to be Pope. To be fair it must be taken into consideration that not so very many Jewish boys go out for these publications. Though that in turn is determined by the fact that they know that there is no or scarce precedent for a Jewish boy being successful. I do know of two instances where two talented Jewish boys in competition for the *Crimson* were very casually dropped, though they were worthwhile, but then, of course, that is open to dispute. To be frank about it, it can be said that the average Jewish boy at Harvard hasn't got a chance of making any of the publications.

"I would say that on the whole Jewish candidates for the athletic teams are not discriminated against. However, I have heard it said and agree that the Jewish athlete would have to be a shade or two better than his non-Jewish rival if he expected to make a certain position, all other things being equal. I, personally, had such an experience. That is the way I would regard it, but then, after all, the coach may have been right. On this question I would give Harvard the benefit of the doubt and say that there is no discrimination.

"The Law School will take in most any college graduate, and it is safe to say that there is no limitation here. At the Medical School, however, there is a different situation due most likely to the limitation of laboratory facilities. At the Business School there are quite a few Jewish boys, and I wouldn't go so far as to say that the Jewish boys were excluded to any degree because I don't know. After all, the records of the admission committees are not open to the public.

"In conclusion I want to say that I feel you are too general in assuming that all the Jewish students are treated the same. Some of them act differently and present themselves so, and to that extent many of them are treated differently, both favorably and unfavorably.

"Another peculiar situation at Harvard is the presence of many wealthy Jewish boys, who very often set themselves aloof from the other Jewish boys and the Gentiles both, or in some cases from the Jews alone. The whole situation at Harvard, I feel, in regard to this problem is quite complex, and very difficult to explain in a letter.

"My personal attitude to this problem has been: the college and its background and tradition are not of my people and race. I am merely there to get an education and let them run it as they want. It would take pages to say the whole thing, so I will let it go.

"There is a decided absence of any overt prejudice—but the attitude toward the Jewish boys as regards the clubs is quite definite, though subtle. The entire attitude is *laisse-faire*. The anti-semitism, if it may be called that, is quite honorable and above board—it is their college and they want to keep it so. That's all.

"To the Jewish boy who wants to remain so and be so, I would say conditions are good. It is only when the Jewish boys seek to leave their natural habitat that what may be called anti-semitism comes into play."

* * *

Curiously enough, some sections of the country where Jewish prejudice is supposedly rampant, present more hospitality in their colleges than those of the North Atlantic states. Thus, ever since the Frank case many Americans have assumed that a distinct and special anti-Jewish bias exists in the South, and naturally this opinion was strengthened on account of Klan activities. But here we may slip into an error. As everybody knows, the Klan was against different groups in different places. Its motivating venom in the South was almost entirely anti-Catholic. A story is told of a Klan parade in Tennessee in which one of the banners carried the slogan "Down with Popery"; and then in a parenthetical clause— "Not anti-Jewish". Very possibly the Klan movement never had any great strength in southern universities. I would not be surprised to find that the Jewish student fares better in many big southern universities than does the Catholic. At any rate, several of the leading football teams in the South have had, as conspicuous members and leaders, Jewish students. For instance, much attention has been given to the fact that in the current season the all-American tackle of the Alabama eleven was Fred Sington, a Jewish student, and this was mentioned so frequently it seems fair to assume that the publicity directors of the college took a particular pride in the prowess of this young man.

Prejudice in the middle western colleges does not seem to be great, nor is it intensive in the southwest. The general rule seems to be that when the number of Jewish students is small, prejudice is not great.

The fiercest feeling has arisen in colleges where there was a large enrollment, and even more particularly where the proportion seemed to be on the increase. The quota system, naturally enough, has been employed chiefly in institutions where this condition existed.

I am told by friends that the lot of the Jewish student at Yale is not easy. Discrimination is somewhat subtle and under cover, and yet my Jewish friends feel that it is real and punishing. It is perhaps unfair to generalize from what may be mere coincidence, but the number of Jewish athletes at Yale has been conspicuously small.

Princeton, on the other hand, as far as teams go, has often been represented on the gridiron or the diamond by Jewish stars, and Jews have on occasion been associated with the annual Triangle Show which is administered largely as an exclusive social activity. Indeed, Princeton is a haven for the pet Jew, but no others need apply. A definite effort seems to have been made to keep up a sort of quota system. It has been the custom of certain deans to solve the problem quite simply by saying to a successful applicant: "We have nothing against you. You have met the scholarship requirements. But we feel that you would not be happy here since you don't seem to be a Princeton type. We advise you to go elsewhere."

* * *

There is no prejudice against Jews in professional sport. In fact, in baseball some managers have gone to unusual lengths to get a Jewish player with a distinctive Jewish name. John McGraw has said on several occasions that a Jewish Babe Ruth, or anybody approximating that great slugger, would be the biggest box-office attraction the game had ever known. He let Rogers Hornsby go in a deal and put in his place a young infielder called Andy Cohen, who had originally come from the University of Alabama. Cohen was only a moderately good ball player, but for a time McGraw's prediction of the drawing power of a Jewish name was fulfilled. He became one of the best known of the new men. Great quantities of stuff were written about him in the papers. He did his autobiography for a syndicate, and wherever the Giants played, some local Jewish group would come to the plate and present Andy with a traveling bag. But in the end Andy was obliged to use some one of these suitcases and travel. Here there was no discrimination, but merely lack of sufficient batting power.

And some four years ago McGraw paid a large price for a player in a bush league largely because he had compiled a good home run record, but even more because his name was Moe Solomon. Solomon received a thorough trial, and then was allowed to drift away again. He couldn't make the grade, and nobody was more disappointed than McGraw, unless maybe it was Solomon.

Other Jewish ball players have been in the big leagues, notably Kling of Chicago. But McGraw was one of the first to place an emphasis on the fact of a player being Jewish.

In the prize ring there was a tendency at one time for Jewish fighters to take Irish names. But that is all changed now, and indeed, Dan Morgan made a fortune for a light heavyweight by inducing him to drop his ring name of Barney Williams, and go back to his own, which happened to be Levinsky. As Battling Levinsky he was, for a long time, a very successful fighter.

In New York many of the most successful fighters have been Jewish. I think off-hand of Benny Leonard, Ruby Goldstein and Al Singer. To be sure, Leonard's own name was Leiner. This was changed simply because in his early preliminary days, an announcer at a Bronx ring could not pronounce the name. But Leonard never evaded the fact that he was Jewish. On the contrary, he was glad to have this known. All these Jewish fighters have managed to command a large and faithful following from such fans as happened to be co-religionists; and, in some cases, they have profited in two ways. It is familiar enough to hear the crowd shout—"Kill the kike," or "Sock the Hebe." But this is not fairly identifiable as race prejudice, for the same crowd would yell just as loudly "Get the Mick," or "Murder the Wop." It may be that there is some distinctly anti-Jewish feeling among fight fans, but even this may come to benefit the pugilist. It was always said of Leach Cross that his chief ability as a drawing card rested in the fact that thousands of people came to every fight in which he participated hoping to see him knocked out. Nevertheless, when he retired from the ring, all the sport pages carried sentimental and appreciative stories of his ring career.

Harry Greb was another famous Jewish fighter, his name being formed by spelling Berg backwards. Jack Kid Berg has not gone to the trouble of making any such transposition, and is one of the best and most popular boxers in the welter-weight and light-weight fields.

One of the early Jewish fighters who made good with almost no inconvenience was Joe Choynski, who later became physical director of the Pittsburgh Athletic Club. And in the older tradition of the ring there appears the famous Mendoza. Jackie Fields, recent welter-weight champion, was born Jakie Finkelstein. The change to Fields was merely a matter of convenience, for he doesn't deny his Jewishness, and, in fact, refuses to carry out training work on the Sabbath.

There are a number of Callahans who were born Cohens, and Morans who started out to be Moskowitzes. But, in the same way, it might be pointed out that Johnny Dundee is an Italian.

There was an Irish boy by the name of Spike Hennessy who ran errands around a New York newspaper office a few years ago, and was an amateur boxer of considerable enthusiasm and ambition. Every Saturday night he went into the ring, and always under the name of "Soldier Jones".

"What's the idea, Spike," he was asked. "Here you have a fine fighting name but you won't use it in the ring. Why do you change it?"

"Gee," said the wise one out of the corner of his mouth, "go in as Spike Hennessy and have everybody yelling 'Kill the Kike?' "

While it has no particular connection with sport, it is curious that in both the theatre and the radio, there is some disposition to get away from obviously Jewish names. Thus, one of the well known announcers was advised by the station which employed him that Ross would be a better name over the air than Rosenthal. And this same station bid furiously with a rival for the services of Jascha Heifetz.

In the theatre the question of name is determined largely by the type of part which is to be played. George Jessel, Eddie Cantor, Al Jolson, Benny Rubin, to name a few, are all avowedly, and even aggressively, Jewish. It's part of the personality by which they prosper. But if any one of them wanted to portray the high-hat young hero of a drawing room comedy, then there would be a certain temptation to cover Jewish ancestry in a Gentile name. Mr. Jolson and Mr. Jessel, to be sure, have both appeared in pictures or plays in which some portion of the performance was not only serious, but actually sob stuff. Yet, even here, there was a racial tie-up as each undertook to carry on such a story as that of the jazz singer who finds it necessary to take the place of his father as cantor at a religious rite. Al Jolson, of course, is known best for his work in black-face. Whether there is any subtle unconscious identification here with membership in another, and even more aggressively oppressed people, I do not know.

I remember once at a New Year's party, a friend of mine was singing "Go Down Moses". A girl sitting on the stairway who could not see the singer, said to me, "Ah, yes, that's magnificent. Only a Negro can sing that song."

"Or," I told her, "an Irish Catholic. His name is MacNamara."

Chapter IV

A LIBERAL EDUCATION

MANNIE LEVY—or maybe his name is Mortimer Lewis—wants to go to college.

The ambitious Jewish people, the vast majority of whom are still among the more recent immigrants, still under the strain of pulling up by the bootstraps from their temporary landing place in New York's East Side, are going after education as does no other group. A study a couple of years ago showed that while in the New York elementary schools there was a thirty percent Jewish enrollment, or a close proportionate parallel to the population, the high schools had fifty-five percent Jewish students. The racial proportion applying for entrance to college doubtless would be even greater. Among the colleges in New York City, Columbia has about 22.5 percent Jews, New York University, although widely credited with having a much larger number, reports 36.53 percent for all departments, and the free public institutions, the College of the City of New York and Hunter College, between eighty and ninety percent.

Mannie Levy has finished preparatory school.

For the sake of the argument, let us allow him high grades and the endorsement of his school principal. Perhaps he is the son of Polish Jewish parents, the first generation born in America, with tenement house manners and a heedless zeal for self-improvement, just graduated from Seward Park High School down at Hester and Essex Streets; or he may have Spanish ancestry, American-born since the Revolution, aristocratic family, wealth, and the superior modern training provided by the Ethical Culture or Walden Schools. Difference in background does not make a great distinction. He is a Jew. He thinks he will just go up to Columbia University. In his own mind, very likely, he rejects City College because "there are too many Jews there."

There was a time when the same objection could have been made to Columbia, as witness the old campus song:

"Oh, Harvard's run by millionaires,
And Yale is run by booze,
Cornell is run by farmers' sons,
Columbia's run by Jews.

So give a cheer for Baxter Street
Another one for Pell,
And when the little sheenies die,
Their souls will go to hell."

But Columbia got busy and wiped away that

slur. In two years shortly after the War, she cut Jewish admissions in incoming classes from forty percent to about half that figure. The enrollment varies now between nineteen and twenty-six percent. Out of nearly five hundred freshmen admitted in the fall of 1929 to Columbia College—the holy of holies department of the university so far as restriction is concerned—there were ninety-two Jews. Barnard College for women, of which, by chance, the wealthy Jew, Jacob H. Schiff, was first treasurer, usually keeps the percentage slightly lower than in Columbia College. Its maximum for Jews is about one-fifth.

Mannie Levy thinks he will go to Columbia. He receives the elaborate eight-page application form and commences filling it out. After asking his name and address, the questionnaire follows up with: "Have you been a student in any other college?" (Columbia College does not freely accept transfers from City College or New York University, where Jews are more numerous;) "Religious affiliation?"; "place of birth?"; "Have you been known by another name or used any variations of your name?"; father's name, occupation, place of birth?; mother's maiden name in full, place of birth?

At the bottom of this first page is space in which Mannie Levy must paste his photograph—a passport photograph as a test of intellectual fitness!

Within the application form, also, there is a detailed, extensive questionnaire for a confidential report on the applicant by his principal. Grades in all school subjects, of course, must be presented.

Then Mannie Levy must take the intelligence examination— the psychological test regarded by Jews as the banner and symbol of exclusion. There is no occasion to emphasize this, however, for an abundance of other perfectly respectable reasons are available to be given for any rejection.

Each applicant from New York also must have a personal interview with a representative of the admissions office.

Furthermore, Columbia says frankly that it favors students from outside the city in preference to the greater number of applicants from within. And the catalogue remarks, "Other things being equal, early applications will receive the preference." One admission official, not at Columbia, enriched this statement with the oral footnote, "with a waiting list, you can do almost anything."

Finally, Mannie Levy must submit to a complete physical examination.

So he does not enter Columbia after all. Regretfully, the university informs him that no provision can be made for him. If he wants to know why, he is given a courteous reason, and under no circumstances is his Jewishness mentioned.

* * *

Mannie Levy looks around then and selects another college. There is the University of Pennsylvania, convenient to New York, of sound scholarship, with no suggestion of arbitrary restriction on admissions. Pennsylvania enrolls a high proportion of Jews and has on the campus a Jewish Student House which is a center of religious and social life, where there is even maintained a kosher dining room, just as in the student house at Columbia.

To Pennsylvania he goes. Immediately, willy nilly, he becomes a member of the second largest political party on the campus, the Jewish party, strong runners-up to the dominant Gentile party. His Jewish friends—his almost by compulsion whether he wants to be clannish or not—proceed to orient him to campus activities and ambitions. They tell him how far he may go, and where he stops.

According to this campus opinion, Mannie Levy may go out profitably for the baseball and basketball teams. There have been Jewish captains in basketball, wrestling and tennis. He may try for *Junto* or *Red and Blue,* the literary magazines. He may become editor of the *Quarterly* or of *Punch Bowl,* the humorous monthly. If he is very good he may become a member of the Dramatic Club. That organization was strongly Jewish a few years ago, and lost status thereby; so the Jewish members themselves adopted a strongly non-semitic policy in electing their successors and restored the club to favor. Debating is his big chance, here as in many other colleges.

On the other hand, his Jewish fellow-students tell Mannie Levy there are some activities on which it is not worth while to waste effort. Unless he is superlatively good, they advise him not to go out for football. They tell of one of the best football players the university ever had, a Jew, only a few seasons back, who warmed the bench almost all of three years. It is hardly worth while to try for the *Pennsylvanian,* the daily newspaper, even though there have been Jews on its staff. He'll never make Mask and Wig, the exclusive club which produces the musical show. Mask and Wig did take a Jew twenty or thirty years ago, and he endures in memory as a permanent exhibit to disprove prejudice. Recently a Jewish student wrote the music for four successive annual Mask and Wig shows and still was not taken into membership.

He shouldn't set his heart on Phi Kappa Beta—the junior honorary society, not Phi Beta Kappa—or Friars or Sphinx, the senior societies. And he can't be elected president of the senior class or a member of the undergraduate council. The foregoing is just campus talk. Perhaps a Jew of requisite fitness and personality could accomplish all these impossibilities. But Mannie Levy is just an average Jewish boy, not a genius or a vastly superior person to disregard the obstacles in his path. He meets this system of fortified positions and mental hazards as he goes to almost any of the big Eastern colleges. And they set him back.

* * *

Thousands of stories will reach the Jewish boy approaching college or already admitted concerning his fellows all over the country who have been snubbed, voted down in student elections, kept off athletic teams, hazed and buffeted.

A Jewish boy at Bowdoin College, Maine, after reporting that he had learned not to attend the dances, summed up the general situation in the phrase that Jewish students were "treated as intellectual equals and social inferiors."

Across the continent at the University of California, a Jewish student at the same time answered an inquiry by writing that he "might enjoy many of the university privileges without being discriminated against, yet there is always a feeling that Jewish students can never attain the highest student body offices no matter how well qualified."

One almost universal discrimination against Jews is, as mentioned in another connection, in the matter of membership in the Greek letter fraternities. Upon reflection, it appears that this may be one of the most extremely mischievous varieties in the entire catalogue. That is, because of its effect upon the non-Jewish student. At this impressionable period in his life, often coming from a rural community where there were no Jews and no prejudices, he is taught that custom excludes Jews from the best and most sacred circles that he is to know. This poison inevitably must tinge the entire life of many an unthinking man.

A chapter at a Southern university made the mistake a few years ago of taking in a personable youth who bore a French-sounding name but who later was found to be Jewish. This fraternity was conscientious. Very regretfully, the brother was asked to return his pin and step out. Some of the fraternities, particularly those of Southern origin, are organized on the pattern of orders of knighthood, with definite constitutional bans against non-Christians.

This great discrimination of fraternities against Jews amounts to more than mere exclusion from a badge and an outlet for the social instinct which appears somewhat glamorous to the incoming freshman. For in many universities, of which Cornell is a good example, the stronger fraternities are political organizations with almost vested interests in certain student offices and appointments. Exclusion from a fraternity automatically bars the student from some of the more important honors. In some colleges the Jewish fraternities have sufficient standing to compete on rather even terms, but not in many.

A tradition at Columbia ordains that the editor of the Spectator, the daily paper, may never be a Jew, although the managing editor usually is.

At one Eastern university some years back was reported the story of a meeting of the rowing crew at the end of the season to elect a captain. The only member of the crew who would be back next year as a senior was a Jew. He was the logical choice for captain. The crew talked it over—the coach really was responsible for the conditioning and strategy of the crew, the coxswain steered the boat, the stroke oar set the pace. What was the use of a captain anyway? So they decided as an experiment not to elect anybody captain that year. The year following, however, they went back to having a captain and an eligible Gentile boy was elected. The crews, generally, next to exclusive clubs, are the final barriers for Jews to climb.

A few years ago a young Jew of prominent family committed suicide at an Eastern university. He had not associated with his fellow Jews and his attempts to make friendships with non-Jews had been rebuffed. He was sensitive and eager to be accepted, seeking all the outward trimmings of the college man—cheering most lustily at the games, wearing the most voluminous raccoon coat. No explanation ever was given—or in fact known—for his sudden suicide. Jewish students said privately that they believed he was beaten by the race barrier. Then they added, "It's so extreme, only a man like Ludwig Lewisohn could use it."

* * *

If our lad Mannie Levy is of the economic class which sends its children to summer camps and private schools, he has learned about prejudice long before he reached college age; for the preps and camps not only discriminate, but they do so frankly, unblushingly, and sometimes, as a matter of valuable advertising, quite ostentatiously. Glancing into this field for a rapid summary, we find the center of discrimination is New York, New Jersey and New England, tapering off toward the South and West. It is more widespread in girls' schools than in boys. The church factor probably is more important here than in almost any other classification, because of the stressing of daily chapel and religious instruction, many schools reporting that "naturally" they do not take Jewish pupils. Small schools are more exclusive than the larger ones.

But exclusion in the schools during the past ten years has greatly declined, just as it has increased in the camps. One school expert remarked, "Ten years ago you could say absolutely that no Jewish pupils ever had been taken at schools of the very highest rank of social standing and expense, such schools as St. Paul's at Concord, N. H., and Lawrenceville, N. J., for boys, and Miss Porter's at Farmington, Conn., or Miss Spence's in New York, for girls. They have taken only a few, at most; but perhaps even those I mentioned have taken one or two." The same authority remarked that Exeter

Academy was an exception. It always has prided itself upon democratic tradition, taking the sons of poor men as well as of the rich, and not raising the barrier entirely against Jews.

Schools which announce that no Jewish pupils are admitted often make exceptions, when urged by an alumnus or influential friend. And those which disclaim exclusion often make entrance requirements in various ways more rigid for them. A quota of from five to fifteen percent is considered about right. When exclusive schools have taken Jews, occasionally ridiculous extreme measures have been employed to conceal the fact.

One of the leading educational advertising agencies generously permitted the authors of this book to see its file of cards submitted by the schools, by which they indicated their facilities, requirements and wishes as to new pupils. For the northeastern section, these cards showed fully one-third of the schools reporting that no Jewish pupils at all are admitted; another third, that they are admitted only with extreme limitations, and one third seemed quite open.

Summer camps more than schools run to all-Gentile or all-Jewish classification. When mixed, they have a quota of about ten or fifteen percent Jewish.

Prejudice, according to experienced camp directors, is spreading westward rapidly. There was a time when all-Jewish camps in the East found it useless to solicit business from families in Cleveland,

Detroit and other Middle Western cities. Mothers would reply, "We'd rather send them to mixed Jewish and Gentile camps nearer home, where the question of prejudice is not raised at all." During the last few years, Jewish children have been coming to the all-Jewish Eastern camps, just because the former receptive Western camps are closed to them.

Another angle of the problem was raised by a Jewish mother who sent her elder children to mixed camps, but the younger ones to the all-Jewish. "We want them to have friends and associations which they can keep," she said. "Making friends with Gentile children means they will grow up and have no set of their own. Gentile friends will draw away from them. So they had better stay among their own people."

* * *

Hundreds of Jewish college students from the East every year go South and to the Middle West, fleeing discrimination. It would be possible to trace to this motive, rather than to money and professionalism, the presence on obscure Southern church college teams of many star Jewish athletes from the North.

Prejudice against Jews in colleges generally may be said to correspond to the area of density of Jewish population. It is strong in the big Eastern colleges—Columbia, Yale, Harvard, Pennsylvania, the New England schools as a whole. Princeton nips the problem in the bud by holding down Jewish admissions far below the percentage in any of the others mentioned. And although there are scores of institutions away from the Jewish centers where there is no overt ban or discrimination, the number seems to be exceedingly small and decreasing where Jews may be accepted in all respects on personal merit.

In the tax-supported state and city colleges the theory of equal opportunity applies strictly so far as admissions are concerned. In many cases, however, it does not go much farther. At the University of Wisconsin recently a college senior and football star shouted during a public controversy, "We are getting so many damned Jews here that something must be done." And at the same university about the same time, a Jewish girl brought suit against Langdon Hall, a dormitory, on the ground that after her application and fee were accepted for admission as a resident, she had been thrown out because she was a Jewess.

The sporting principle that the race is to the swift applies only with reservations. The practical attitude in many cases seems to be that preferably the Jew ought not to run at all, but, running, if he happens to prove the most swift he should not get the blue ribbon.

Endowed institutions—far the largest class, founded by religious denominations or other private groups, controlled now by church, alumni, or board not responsible to the whole public, accepting gladly the contributions of Jewish philanthropists—generally are less receptive to Jewish enrollment. Colleges everywhere since the war have been faced with more applicants for admission than they could receive. The practice in many cases is to let the inevitable exclusion fall with unequal burden upon the Jews. After all the Gentiles are seated, in effect, Jews may have the vacancies.

Since the colleges were endowed, American life has changed. The machine age has dawned; the population has been unbalanced by myriad waves of foreign immigration. Many of the colleges still cling to a policy dating back to their original design of turning out New England clergymen. It is the Ku Klux policy that democratic education be reserved for native-born, Protestant Nordics. One may easily rationalize such a practice by considering that the colleges have been identified for years with a certain product—"Harvard men", "Princeton men" being supposedly recognizable types—and they wish to continue delivering the kind expected of them.

They do not consider the Jewish applicant good raw material. It certainly has been true for years that the majority of Jewish students were the sons of self-sacrificing immigrant parents. Many of them sought to go through on a minimum expenditure, most of them living at home and not mixing in dormitory life, often uncommonly eager and argumentative in class—fair targets for social snobbery immediately, before real points of demerit or merit became manifest.

In a policy of Jewish restriction, the colleges unquestionably have the tacit support of the largest single group of the population. Such a policy is assumed by many without thought as to unfairness. However, it is nothing less than a silent cultural assent to the Klan crudity that "this is a white man's country." If the issue were carried into the open, many would dismiss it with, "I don't like Jews; I don't want to associate with them," assured that the "good Jew" is an exception who may be granted equitable relief individually. This attitude is perfectly satisfactory to any mind—except one which resents being stigmatized as "prejudiced."

It is to such complacent acceptance that H. G. Wells spoke when he said:

> "I am convinced myself that there is no more evil thing in this present world than race prejudice, none at all! I write deliberately—it is the worst single thing in life now. It justifies and holds together more baseness, cruelty and abomination than any sort of error in the world."

* * *

The colleges themselves as great liberal institutions of the higher learning, would not plead guilty to any charge of race prejudice or discrimination. They do not mention the word quota. No applicant is told that his Jewishness is the reason for his rejection.

The less pretentious schools sometimes show more honesty. A business college in Boston began rejecting Jews and explained with perfect logic that it guaranteed positions to all graduates and, since many firms did not employ Jews, it would not commit itself to finding places for them. Even more open was the Katharine Gibbs School for secretarial training in New York, which wrote:

> March 17, 1928.
>
> "My dear Miss Cohen:
>
> We are sorry to inform you that it is our policy not to accept students of Jewish nationality. We are, therefore, not forwarding our catalogue unless we hear from you further.
>
> Very truly yours,
> (Signed) Assistant Director."

A well-known woman's college in a recent catalogue made one of the frankest statements of restriction against Jews. It said simply that only fifteen percent of the student body would be Jewish.

Second-hand testimony, but not third-hand, concerning Colgate University came out at a summer conference for the promotion of better racial relations held at Eaglesmere, Pennsylvania. A representative from Colgate in open meeting quoted his dean as saying there never would be more than six Jews in the university at once. If the charge of anti-Semitism should be raised, the six would be an adequate exhibit to disprove it. At the same time the number would be so small as to be negligible.

The usual practice of the colleges is silence, evasion, and denial. The percentage varies even between departments of the same university, usually being larger in the professional schools. In medical colleges, much sought after by Jewish applicants, restriction is particularly bitter. The medical college aspect is a separate large subject. The extent of prejudice on the campus varies from year to year, depending upon the dominant minds among students or the aggressiveness of administrators. A strongly liberal college one year may leap suddenly to the other extreme.

Prejudice against Jews in colleges today, apparently, is not nearly so outspoken as a few years ago. It reached its peak of frankness about 1922 when Henry Ford was waging his campaign of hate, when the Klan power was un-exposed, at the time President Lowell at Harvard was proposing his system of restriction. Columbia University, under probably the most active pressure from Jewish applicants of any American university and now steadfastly keeping the number within a quota, is one of the best examples of silent exclusion. For a long time, it seems probable, President Nicholas Murray Butler of Columbia and President A. Lawrence Lowell of Harvard will be ranked together as the leaders of the movement for educational restriction of Jews.

* * *

Surveys by two different Jewish agencies acting independently have just made available for the present volume a large and reliable collection of data on the status of Jewish students in colleges all over the United States.

The most comprehensive of all studies of race prejudice in education was made about four years ago by a Jewish intercollegiate student organization, based upon answers to questionnaires by Jewish students themselves. It is given publication here for the first time.

First the institutions were divided into four classes, depending upon the degree of anti-Jewish feeling reported. The rating, taking the students' word for it, is as follows:

Those with no anti-Jewish feeling whatever—University of Alabama, Connecticut State, Hunter, Lehigh, Louisiana State, College of the City of New York, Newcomb, University of North Carolina, Philadelphia Textile, Rensselaer, Union College,

Utah, Vanderbilt, Vermont, Worcester Polytechnic, Cooper Union.

Slight anti-Jewish feeling—Boston University, University of California, Carnegie Tech., University of Colorado, Georgia, Massachusetts Institute of Technology, University of Missouri, Nebraska, Northeastern, Pennsylvania, Purdue, Syracuse, Tulane, Washington University, Western Reserve, Wisconsin.

Moderate—Bellevue Medical College, University of Buffalo, University of Chicago, Dickinson, Georgia Tech., Harvard, Indiana, Lowell Textile, Long Island College, Michigan, New York University, Osgood Hall Law, University of Pittsburgh, Rutgers, Toronto, Tufts.

Pronounced—Adelphi, Armour Institute, Case School of Applied Science, Cincinnati, Columbia, Cornell, Johns Hopkins, Illinois, Kansas, McGill, Minnesota, Northwestern, Ohio State, Penn State, Texas, Virginia, Washington and Lee, Yale.

The inclusion of the University of Virginia among those exhibiting pronounced anti-Jewish feeling is interesting by contrast to the famous letter which Thomas Jefferson, founder of the university, wrote in 1826 to Isaac Harby, saying:

> "I have thought it a cruel addition to the wrongs which that injured sect have suffered, that their youth should be ex-

cluded now from instruction in science afforded to all others in our public seminaries, by imposing upon them a course of theological reading which their consciences do not permit them to pursue; and in the university lately established here, we have set the example of ceasing to violate the rights of conscience by any injunctions on the different sects respecting their religion."

Returning to the survey, one finds this analysis of student reports:

> "Manifestations of anti-Jewish feeling took the following forms: slurring remarks, social aloofness, exclusion from honorary fraternities, glee clubs, managership of social organizations; difficulty of election to honorary fraternities, discrimination in campus politics, exclusion of Jewish fraternities from inter-fraternity boards; offensive jokes in student publications and student dramatics, general unfriendliness.
>
> "This falls into two groups: 1. Social aloofness of non-Jewish students; 2. Tendency of non-Jewish students to act as a party in selection of men to fill positions of

> responsibility. It would appear from the answers that practically all Jewish students were ostracized socially. The most flagrant manifestations reported are:
>
> "1. Failure on the part of non-Jewish fraternities to invite Jewish fraternities to social functions, such as dances.
>
> "2. Segregation of Jewish girl students from non-Jewish students in some of the dormitories; e.g., Ohio State University.
>
> "3. Admonitions given to non-Jewish girl students not to associate with Jewish young men; e.g., Universities of Michigan and Nebraska.
>
> "It must be borne in mind, however, that only about one-fourth of the institutions covered by this survey reported any serious cases of anti-Jewish feeling at all, and in a number of instances this was based on the testimony of only one or a small number of students."

The foregoing report assembled data from sixty-six different institutions in which there were reported 236,395 students in all, of whom 10.72 percent were Jewish. More than one-third of the Jews were enrolled in institutions in New York City. The survey showed that Jews constituted 11.42 percent of all the male students and 9.25 percent of the female. Apparently a larger number of Jewish boys in proportion to Gentiles go to college than Jewish girls.

The Jewish students contributed 7.75 percent of the members of athletic teams in their institutions or considerably below their proportionate quota, but 19.55 percent of the managers of campus publications and 22.46 percent of the debating team members. The Jewish membership on athletic teams was particularly low in institutions where a large number did not live on the college campus but commuted from their homes.

The survey reported that 15.87 percent of the total 2,306 chapters of fraternities and sororities in these institutions were Jewish. In only fifteen of the sixty-six institutions did any non-Jewish fraternity or sorority admit Jewish members. Jewish fraternity chapters, however, were admitted to membership in the general pan-Hellenic councils of all but eleven of the institutions.

After this survey, the report brought in various recommendations summarized as follows:

"Jewish students should bravely face the fact that to a certain extent anti-Jewish feeling will always exist in the college, and that the degree and intensity of this feeling will be in direct proportion to the outward manifestations of their Jewish characteristics; in other words, to the extent of the outward and visible difference between the Jewish and the non-Jewish students.

"It follows therefore, that there are two things we should strive for: first, to eradicate the merely apparent and fortuitous traits and characteristics which set the Jew apart and which have no real basis in the Jewish character and teachings; second, to cultivate real Jewish characteristics, in order that the clash between the two groups shall be based on realities, and therefore, tend to yield results which may be of benefit to both sides."

* * *

A second survey, made in the spring of 1930 by the *Jewish Daily Bulletin,* based likewise upon questions answered by Jewish students, brought replies from thirty-six out of about one hundred and fifty institutions queried. More than half reported there was no anti-Jewish feeling or practically no discrimination except as to fraternity membership. The replies appear to be most optimistic, until one considers the institutions which are missing. Those reporting no prejudice or at most only slight outbursts are given here. The figures indicate the percentage of Jewish enrollment reported:

Hunter College, about 85 percent; Vassar, 4½ percent; Tufts College, 15 percent; University of Maryland, less than 10 percent; Vanderbilt, 7 percent; Tulane, 7 percent; University of Denver, 12½ percent; University of Iowa, about 3.3 percent; Iowa

State College, three-tenths percent; University of Maine, 4 percent; University of Nebraska, 2 percent; University of South Carolina, 4 or 5 percent; University of Utah, 2 percent; University of Arizona, 2 percent; Purdue, 2 percent; Massachusetts Agricultural College, 5 percent; Baylor University, 8 Jews out of 2,600 students; Florida State College for Women, 2 percent; Oregon State Agricultural College, 19 Jews out of 3,500 students; University of Louisville, 8 or 9 percent; University of Montana, 5 Jews out of 1,500 students; University of Indiana, 3½ percent; Antioch, 3 percent.

These names contain less contradiction of the report of three years previous than might reasonably have been expected, considering the rapid changes in campus personnel. Although they are a different group of colleges, it is noticeable that none of those previously reported as manifesting pronounced prejudice here is absolved.

The most encouraging in the group is one of the big corn belt universities, where a student wrote:

> "The inter-fraternity ball admits, without hesitation or deliberation, members of these Jewish groups. Some of the more popular members receive bids to almost every dance given by Gentile fraternities or sororities. In our chapter we have made it a practice, for example, to have our Gentile

> friends as guests at lunch or dinner. There have been, to my knowledge, no refusals of invitations. At a time when one of the biggest fraternities on the campus was entertaining representatives from its chapters in other colleges and was pressed for room, we were called upon to house several boys. I bring this up as a specific example of the friendliness that exists among Jews and Gentiles."

However, the same student writes:

> "It is generally known among Jewish boys that they cannot hope to 'date' girls affiliating with the so-called better sororities. Should a pledge of one of these larger sororities have a date with a Jewish boy she is threatened with the loss of pledgeship upon repetition. Should the girl be an upper-classman, she is criticized by her sisters. Perhaps this is best after all, though."

The letter makes the perfectly sensible explanation of the prevailing good fellowship by saying:

> "Then, too, a great proportion of the Gentile students are drawn from the small

> towns of this and surrounding states. Is it not logical to assume that since a great many of these students have not known anti-Semitism in their home towns they will not, immediately after coming to university, suddenly become victims of this prejudice?"

Another of the state universities, from which a report of "no prejudice" was made, qualified it with this statement:

> "There have been and are Jewish students on the athletic teams, but the feeling is widespread that the Jewish students must be above the average in ability to get in. Between a Gentile and a Jew of the same ability, the Gentile will get the position. Jews have been entering athletics in increasing numbers, and speaking generally have received fair treatment.
>
> "There is a case at present in which I am interested. J. S., a fraternity brother of mine, has been reporting regularly for varsity basketball. He was chosen a member of the squad. Players of much less ability have been sent into the game. At first the squad consisted of eleven members. On out of town trips thé coach took

> ten and left J. S. at home. The squad has now been increased to thirteen. On the last out of town trip the coach took twelve and again J. S. stayed at home."

Antioch College, with its unique system of dividing study with work in industrial plants, presents a more complicated exhibit. A student wrote from there:

> "Unfortunately, Jewish students on the job sometimes do meet with anti-semitic prejudice. I was once told by the head of the personnel department at the college that the chief reason I was discharged from a job in 1927 (naming the employer) was that the manager of the plant was the former head of the Ku Klux Klan in that city. On another job that summer I was told that there was a slight feeling against me on the part of some of the other employees.
>
> "That is all I have experienced. It is my belief, though, that the personnel department is careful in giving jobs to Jewish students to see that they will not be at a disadvantage while on the job.
>
> "Summing up, there is on the campus no anti-semitic prejudice but in most cases

a feeling of comradeship. On the job there is without doubt some prejudice, which consideration sometimes enters into the awarding of jobs to Jewish students."

* * *

Warmth and sunshine seem to come out and soothe the harassed Jewish student as one reads most of the foregoing reports from the 1930 survey. There is definitely a lighter side to the picture, and it might just as well be looked at here, before turning again to the search for prejudice.

A Jew was awarded a Rhodes Scholarship to Oxford from Reed College, Oregon, in the fall of 1929, and another about the same time was even elected captain of the basketball team at Yale.

The Roman Catholic colleges as a class usually have escaped the charge of anti-semitism, not only those such as Georgetown and Notre Dame where there are few Jews, but also Fordham where the Jewish enrollment is large. Furthermore Jewish professors report that they have a better chance to obtain positions in Catholic colleges. If a Catholic scholar is not available, there seems no objection to a Jew; he is preferred to a Protestant.

A student in an evening law class at Fordham, in the Bronx Division, commented on his experiences: "Jewish students represent twenty-five percent of the total. The relationship between Jewish and non-

Jewish students is pleasant, amiable, I might even say cordial. The professors are absolutely fair and impartial without even the slightest trace of anti-semitic prejudice. In the one course taught by a priest, the Jewish students on the whole received much higher ratings than the non-Jewish."

Among the more cosmopolitan universities, Chicago probably has exhibited less prejudice against Jews in recent years than any. There is no restriction on entrance, and many Jews attend. They have held virtually every undergraduate distinction except the presidency of the senior class and offices in the residence hall organizations. Jews are numerous on publications, in the sought-after dramatic club, Blackfriars, and in athletics, even attaining the captaincy of the football team. There are Jewish fraternities for men, clubs for women, and outstanding Jews are taken occasionally into the non-Jewish fraternities. A recent covert movement among girl students to vote the Jewish members out of the residence halls was squelched.

Before one becomes too comfortable, however, in this view of good will, the limitations of the picture should be examined. Glancing again at the survey, one notices that it contains little data about the older colleges of the Northeast, located in the highly congested Jewish sections of the country where pressure for admission is strongest and prejudice, traditionally, is most bitter.

Examining the institutions reporting no prejudice, one is struck by the small percentage of Jewish students there. All but two have less than ten percent Jews; more than two-thirds have less than five percent. It would appear in this view that for the University of Montana, for example, to boast to Columbia about having no anti-Jewish prejudice would be exactly the same as for Amherst to preen itself before the University of California upon its freedom from anti-Japanese feeling.

One may say almost without qualification that there is only slight anti-Jewish prejudice if any in colleges such as the College of the City of New York and Hunter where Jews are so numerous as by their very bulk to smother the Gentiles, and likewise in those where Jews are so few as to be scarcely noticed. Where the Jewish enrollment is so small that there is no possibility of considering Jews as a class, they frequently get along, as individuals, almost entirely on merit. There the personally acceptable Jew may win high position and popularity. Where there are a large number of Jewish students, the individual almost always faces strong arbitrary prejudices. For intervals it may be dormant; then it flares up again in the most respected institutions, operating with extreme blindness and cruelty, seldom distinguishing between individuals.

* * *

New York City's institutions have distinctive problems and systems which have not yet been discussed, and they constitute the best opportunity in the United States for observation of Jewish students and prospective students.

Columbia's machine for regulating the flow of Jewish students through its classrooms is one of the most elaborate ever devised. Armed with its eight-page blank, its talk of scholarship standards, its personal interviews, psychological tests, physical examinations, and passport photograph requirements, Columbia can select exactly the applicants it desires, keep the Jewish quota down to the fractional percentage it may determine, and defy any one to slip by unnoticed. With this minute sifting for good material and testing for young scholars of promise, if Columbia fails to produce the bulk of the nation's future leaders, it will be a discouraging blow to human foresight.

The analysis of Columbia's system already given in the case of Mannie Levy is admittedly less than just to the university. The plan is not aimed entirely at Jews, but is really intended to select the best possible material according to Columbia's standards. The physical examination is a health measure, usually performed by the applicant's own physician.

Columbia's position is that it is not a local institution but national. With a capacity in Columbia

College of from one thousand, eight hundred to two thousand students, the administration seeks to obtain at least half its students from outside the City of New York. It wants its campus atmosphere to reflect more than the self-centered metropolitan point of view. Furthermore, it has the real-estate rental problem of extensive dormitories. There are about four applicants for each possible admission to the college. Approximately half are eliminated by scholarship requirements; the others are disposed of by the various hurdles mentioned.

The university was founded as an institution of the Episcopal Church. This connection it still retains, being, as described irreverently, "a branch of Trinity Church." However, a Jew, Gershom Mendez Seixas, was one of the original incorporators when Kings College became Columbia College. After an unbroken interval of a century, another Jew was elected to the board of trustees, Chief Justice Benjamin N. Cardozo.

But if Columbia College is national and Episcopal, its branch in Brooklyn, Seth Low Junior College, is local and Jewish. Many rejected applicants for Columbia College go there and are admitted. The Jewish enrollment at Seth Low is about eighty percent. Not only does it draw heavily from Brooklyn but from other parts of the city. Jewish students from the Bronx come down the Broadway subway past 116th Street, the station for Columbia University, and ride forty-five minutes longer over to Seth Low. Jewish students living on Morningside Heights next door to Columbia meet incoming student throngs as they take their train at the 116th Street station to go where there is no discouragement to Jewish enrollment. This desire of Jews elsewhere in the city to attend Columbia, as represented by Seth Low, may account for the fact that it has a higher Jewish percentage than the almost entirely Brooklyn institution, Long Island University, where the Jewish enrollment is given as about seventy-five percent.

After students complete their junior college work at Seth Low, they may be admitted to the Morningside Heights institution to work for their degree—but not to Columbia College. They are taken in as "university undergraduates", usually having afternoon classes, getting their diplomas from the University direct. Columbia College is protected.

Columbia's system of exclusion finds no counterpart at the College of the City of New York. Since the late 1890's the Jew has outnumbered the Gentile here. No question as to race or religion is asked upon entrance—a unique omission. It has been called often "the Jewish College of America."

Even at City College, however, there are Greek letter fraternities of the minority which customarily do not initiate Jews. And a charge of unfairness to Jews was made in 1927 in the extremely Jewishconscious periodical, *The Reflex*. It was, of course, promptly denied.

In the long ago past, however, there was a clear case of discrimination at City College. Soon after the Civil War the college president, General Alexander Webb, refused to excuse Jewish students from class on religious holidays, except upon condition that they forfeited their grades on those days. This naturally handicapped them for scholarship honors. There was a protest, and the trustees revoked the ruling.

The college never has had a Jewish president, although Henry Leipziger, a Jew, once was acting president. The present chairman of the board of trustees is Moses J. Stroock, a Jew, and Jews outnumber either Catholics or Protestants on the board.

Although there are about one hundred and fifty Jews on the faculty or nearly half the total teaching staff, only five have the rank of full professor. Six are associate professors. Two of the five professors are heads of departments. All five are men of exceptional attainments. The percentage of Jews in the lower orders, the instructorships and assistantships, is much higher than among the more desirable positions. Even in a friendly college, the openings for Jewish professors are distinctly limited. One Jewish professor, not counted among the five, has renounced his religion and become a Roman Catholic. The registrar who controls admissions and keeps the records of students dropped for bad scholarship is a Jew.

New York University, besieged just as Columbia and City College by a numerous and ambitious Jewish population, stands between the other two as to enrollment percentages. The psychological test is utilized at the University Heights branch, or officially, the University College of Arts and Pure Science. The catalogue announces that it "has selective admission. The selection of applicants is made on the basis of high school record and such personnel and intelligence tests as may be required. . . . Special arrangements will be made for applicants living at a distance."

However, any charge of extreme discrimination on admission at N. Y. U. is not borne out by figures on religious percentages supplied by Henry G. Arnsdorf, the registrar. For the year 1928–29 in all departments Jews were reported as 36.53 percent, Protestant 24.36, Roman Catholic 19.45 and those of no religious preference 19.5. One may assume that some part of the latter classification also was Jewish.

The Jewish representation appears even larger in figures for the more conspicuous departments. Here the official percentage of Jewish enrollment was reported as: University College of Arts and Pure Science 54.3; Washington Square College 63.4; College of Dentistry 77.4; Law 67.9; Engineering

26.15; Medicine 69.7; Commerce 22.8; Fine Arts 9.8; Graduate School of Business Administration 3.5.

N. Y. U. represents probably the most striking dualism, a house divided against itself, to be found in the academic world. Washington Square College is the entirely urban, fermenting, non-restricted, non-collegiate, profit-earning knowledge factory which houses the world's largest numerical group of undergraduate Jewish students. Upon the other hand is University Heights, its wooded campus surrounded by the city but attempting to maintain conventional college atmosphere and spirit, erecting the barrier of "selective admissions", operating by endowment rather than earning its way, about one-twelfth the size of its down-town sister, and still the darling, hope and pride of the administration. The Heights is the last stand of the Old Guard.

It is not by accident that N. Y. U. has the best football team in the city. The team is part of the setting at the Heights. And this again is a difference from Washington Square. The University Heights students attend the games and yell to the cheer leaders' beckon. The Jewish boys from downtown go too, but as unsentimentally as an average New Yorker might watch the Giants play baseball.

New York University introduced "selective admission" at University Heights in September, 1919.

The university's attitude was explained publicly in a report by Dean Archibald L. Bouton in December, 1922, when he said:

> "We were at that time threatened, as you well know, with nothing less than the immediate disintegration of our college body as it was then constituted at University Heights. . . . It is still true as it was in 1919, and in this metropolitan environment it will long be true, that our chief problems center in students of Russian, Polish and Central European parentage, most of them the sons of immigrants in the first generation.
>
> "At present approximately forty percent of our student body is Protestant, thirty percent is Catholic, and thirty percent is Jewish. . . . We do not exclude students of any race or national origin because they are foreign, but whenever the student body is found to contain elements from any source in such proportions as to threaten our capacity for assimilating them to the standards of national life, which, as an educational institution, we hold, then in the interest of our functions as a college, as we interpret it, we seek by selection to restore the balance."

The reverse side of this picture is reported in a letter published in the *Nation,* July 12, 1922, signed by Joseph Girdansky. It is quoted here for whatever face value it may possess. Says the letter:

> "It was two years ago or possibly three in the merry month of May that class elections of the junior year were held.
>
> "My brother, a Jewish student of irreproachable reputation as well as an athlete of sorts, was elected president of the junior class (the first time in N. Y. U. history that a Jew received that honor in the College of Arts and Sciences). With him other Jews were elected to a majority of the class offices. Whether this was good judgment or not, they were of the class and were elected by and for the class.
>
> "When the elections were announced, the faculty—mind you, the faculty—called off the elections, using the pretext that, first, the officers elected were Bolshevists (a popular epithet at that time); secondly, that there had been ballot-stuffing; and thirdly, fourthly and fifthly, that the elections were null and void. To add insult to injury, the officers (Jewish) were threatened with expulsion for the offense of being elected.

"As an alumnus of some athletic prominence or notoriety, I was requested to interview the Dean (Bouton) and I did. We had a long and startlingly frank talk. The worthy dean (and he really is that, in spite of his dilemma) finally agreed that Bolshevism and ballot-stuffing were not the issue—that it was simply a Jewish question—that, whereas in my days, about 1907, with a Jewish percentage of students of about two to four, the percentage now 'threatened' to be over fifty and would be if not restrained. I am not going to bore you with our conversation, but he concluded that after a lot of deliberation the authorities had decided to add another examination to the list of entrance exams (viz., 'the psychological exam employed by Columbia.') I am quoting the dean's exact language. This was intended merely as a means of barring from admission to the college any Jew they thought undesirable and to make sure that the total number admitted would be about ten or fifteen percent. The general name given this procedure was 'Americanization plans', also a popular term of that day.

"As a result of my threat to expose this state of affairs, at a time when the university was making appeals for an endowment fund, the dean promised that if I would wait until the fall, the class election would be settled to my satisfaction. In the fall, when a good many of the Jewish students in that class left University Heights to enter medical school, either new elections were held or appointments were made by the faculty, with the result that non-Jews held all the important posts.

"At the time I interviewed the only Jewish member of the board of trustees, Percy S. Straus. He had not heard of the new Americanization plan, but agreed that it would be desirable to limit the percentage of incoming Jewish students at the college."

* * *

Eastern colleges outside New York City, while not receiving the same large numbers of Jewish applicants for admission, still find themselves likely to become predominantly Jewish in student body unless they exercise firm selective powers. Reports of discrimination either on admission or in the course of campus life could be gathered from almost all these institutions.

In passing it may be noted that the University of Michigan, pretty safely distant yet from the area of intensive Jewish settlement, already is armed with an admission questionnaire even more voluminous than Columbia's. It includes "I. Q. tests". Examination of it, though, does not suggest any such definite pointing toward discovery of a particular race as in the Columbia document. Michigan has not been approached in great numbers by Jews, and they make up only a small percent of its students. Some have been mighty in athletics, and very popular.

Rutgers University at New Brunswick, N. J., was the subject of one of the most recent complaints of prejudice. The charge was that Jewish graduates of high schools in New Brunswick, Perth Amboy, Elizabeth, and other New Jersey cities were excluded or threatened with rejection because of their race. Affidavits making the assertions were filed with the Board of Regents of the state by Julius Kass, a Jewish attorney and alumnus of the university, in October, 1930. And there the matter rests. Quoting from this sworn account of the lawyer's interview with Dean Metzger, admittedly *ex parte,* we find:

> "Dean Metzger admitted frankly that very few Jewish students had been admitted this year. He said the reason only thirty-three were admitted was in order to 'equalize the proportion' and that the committee on admissions had been instructed by the trustees that Rutgers wasn't to be made

> 'denominational'. He further said, 'Rutgers got away from the old Dutch denominationalism years ago and we do not wish it to become predominantly Jewish now. . . .
>
> "I then asked Dean Metzger to assume a case in which a Jewish student in the upper quarter of the class in preparatory school and a non-Jewish student who was in the lower three-quarters of his class both applied for admission at a time when the so-called 'Jewish quota' had been filled. Which would be admitted? Dean Metzger answered, without hesitation, 'The non-Jewish student.' "

The affidavit also contains the undisputed assertion that after eight out of a group of nine boys from the New Brunswick Senior High School had been refused by Rutgers, while eighteen non-Jewish boys were admitted, a protest was made to the superintendent of schools of New Brunswick. Then, says the affidavit, "I understand that Rutgers was notified that if these boys were not admitted, Rutgers would not be permitted to send practice teachers to New Brunswick High School. . . . Political pressure was brought to bear and shortly thereafter, I was informed that the eight boys had been admitted."

Dean Metzger when queried about the incident,

replied, "There is no discrimination against any student at Rutgers."

Syracuse University, being conveniently located to New York City, faces the constant possibility of a disproportionate invasion of Jewish students from the city. It is among the universities in which dread and prejudice seem to be almost constantly smouldering. Occasionally it breaks into the newspapers in unwelcome fashion upon this point. The loudest protest came in February, 1923, when it was reported that three members of a special committee of the Senior Council had recommended that the authorities be asked "to rid the hill of Jews." They proposed a gradual reduction in the quota and a policy of discouragement. The chancellor of the university immediately rebuked the group, and demanded and obtained a complete retraction of the resolution. The number of Jewish students then in the university was estimated at about fifteen percent. The present rate of admissions is about ten percent. Syracuse, of course, is a private, church-supported institution, and it stresses religion in the unusually searching and extensive questions on its entrance application blank.

In a letter of two years ago a Jewish student at Cornell, who was not at all an impersonal witness, testified to the view of life there as gathered by one particular young man. The Jewish enrollment is about twelve percent. The student wrote:

"Cornell is rightfully considered one of the most liberal of universities, in the respect that the faculty is very liberal in its attitude toward Jewish students. Unfortunately, its students, some of them, have a very different attitude, one often of deliberate prejudice and discrimination. It is due to this attitude that certain clubs, honorary societies and publications not only do not admit Jews to membership but also publish cartoons and articles derogatory to Jews, and adopt a semi-public attitude of mild anti-Semitism that influences campus opinion against Jews.

"In some competitions (for publications) Jews are frankly discouraged and advised to drop out. In my own case I have been told that it was 'a damn shame' that I was Jewish, but it was 'the policy of the board,' not to elect Jewish men, just as it was the policy of the board to publish those objectionable cartoons."

Cornell, however, has made definite progress toward liberalism, according to another student, Saul R. Kelson, last year. He provided the authors of this book with a comprehensive summary of conditions—which he later expanded into an excellent magazine article—reporting little overt discrimination. If some of his philosophy sounds a trifle like sour grapes, it reveals at least a student who organized his own life successfully and is not suffering. He said:

> "In 1926 it was exceptional and triumphant for a Jew to make the *Sun.* Many declare that prejudice then was the reason, and point out a number of questionable decisions in various competitions. Now the name Loeb or Altman in the masthead is ordinary.
>
> "The distasteful jibes and cartoons which appear from time to time on its pages indicate that the *Widow,* the so-called humorous publication, is unmistakably anti-Semitic. That the *Widow* will take no Jews is well-known, both from the absence of Jewish board members for something like the past twenty-five years and from the admission of various editors. The *Widow* is admittedly a social organization which attempts to maintain an esoteric position by excluding Jews, foreign students, and some independents. The Jews have ceased to pay attention to it, and the wiser ones do not waste time contending for its positions."

He rambles through other activities, commenting:

"An instance of apparent discrimination against a Jew eligible to Tau Beta Pi, honorary engineering society, is problematical.

"Honorary societies are, on the whole, fair to Jews. In Sphinx Head, the senior honorary society, there is an equitable proportion, determined solely by the number who have made their place in activities. Until two years ago, Quill and Dagger, the other senior honorary, had admitted no Jews. Today, the qualified Jew is practically certain to be selected by one of the two.

"The social and drinking and professional clubs to which we come next are frequently hotbeds of prejudice. Forming as rapidly as new keys and scarf pins can be designed, these clubs tend to breed snobbery. Though they mask behind a label of 'honorary', these closed corporations select cronies on the basis of their potential alcoholic content or something of the sort. No Jew ought to feel slighted if he is not selected. To a Jewish 'big man on the hill,' few doors are barred unless he happens to be personally obnoxious in some way or other.

"I have heard a great deal of complaint

> from Jewish students that the Cornell employment agency discriminates against them. Investigation makes it clear that whatever discrimination is displayed arises not from the agency itself, but from the wish of various employers to secure non-Jewish help. Some fraternities do not care to have Jewish waiters; a Jewish fraternity, I am told, is among the number."

Princeton University has come down as a stronghold of the culture which does not recognize Jews, and yet it has avoided discourtesy or outburst in connection with them. It sits on its hill in its own little town off the railroad between New York and Philadelphia, paying no attention to either, reasonably free from their problems and saying nothing.

Princeton has virtually no Jewish problem, because it has a negligible number of Jews. None of the big Eastern colleges has so few. A number of the faculty in conversation, not of course expressing the university's policy as its official spokesman, said there was a quota based upon the percentage of Jews in the United States—something less than four percent. The same proportion holds in the Graduate College. An instructor in the Graduate College remarked that he had not known one Jew accepted or admitted there within the past four years who had a characteristically Jewish name.

Yet the university has no such machinery for sifting applicants as has Columbia. Its system is to let the preparatory schools do the disagreeable work. A vast majority of Princeton freshmen come from the prep schools; the number varies from seventy-five to ninety percent. Most of the fashionable private schools have quotas; some refuse Jews altogether. Drawing from such sources, Princeton is able to side-step almost completely. The strong Southern element at Princeton is another element of safety, making the risk of Jewish immigration much less than if students were drawn heavily from New York.

Once admitted, according to Princeton students, Jews do not have a bad time. They would not be taken into the Ivy, Tiger, Cottage, Cap and Gown or other of the more swanky student clubs. Some clubs have written laws which bar Jews. But others take in a select few. From six to ten Jews altogether who are admitted to the clubs is a fair average. They are not taken, as members, by the Triangle Club, the exclusive organization which stages the annual musical show. In athletics the Jew may go as far as his ability carries him, and in general campus activity he may find a place. The general impression is that Jews are undesirable, but individuals may be given a chance.

* * *

The New England colleges as a class receive

fewer applications from Jewish students than those in New York City, admit a smaller quota, and in many cases are charged with practicing a more rigid social boycott.

Dartmouth College probably is the leading example in the United States of a geographical assignment of quotas for the sake of obtaining a diversified student body. The alumni in various sections are active in interviewing and reporting on the fitness of prospects. Dartmouth also has a waiting list.

A summary of conditions at Dartmouth which is sketchy but fair in intention, written by a professor there in a personal letter in the spring of 1930, is as follows:

> "Discrimination, if it exists, is kept under cover. For the past several years the Jews admitted to the freshman class have made an average of about seven percent. The theory of admission is, I believe, that the various segments of the population should be represented in each class. So they try to get in a certain percentage of far westerners, middle westerners, southerners, and so on.
>
> "The number of Jews on the faculty is small. Off-hand I can think of but three. Choosing new men is a departmental mat-

ter. I don't believe any department has an official policy concerning Jews. I believe in our department an outstanding Jew would be accepted. But if a Jew and Gentile of roughly similar qualifications were being considered, undoubtedly the Gentile would be given preference.

"A few Jews belong to Gentile fraternities, but in general they are not taken. A Deke explained the situation thusly: one man can exert an effective blackball. If one Jew is taken in, he may refuse to pass anybody else unless some of his Jewish friends are admitted. No fraternity wants the reputation of having a number of Jews as members. Q.E.D. This Deke himself rooms with a Jew who is an Alpha Delta Phi, one of the baby trinity at Dartmouth. The Alpha Delt Jew is not an athlete.

"I asked the manager of the *Dartmouth,* the college daily, about Jews on the publication. He said he was chary about having them on publication boards. Again his argument was that one on the board meant more later on, for the board chooses its successors. The *Dartmouth Pictorial* had become Jewish in this way."

Brown University in February, 1928, was the scene of a slight flurry over the refusal of the authorities to permit the organization of Jewish fraternities. The incident became public over the exclusion of a chapter of the Jewish fraternity, Pi Lambda Phi. A protest was made by Louis Marshall, president of the American Jewish Committee. Dr. W. H. P. Faunce, president of the university, replied:

> "Nothing worse could happen to our colleges than to have secret societies established along political or religious or racial lines. I should strongly object to a Baptist fraternity at Brown, although I am a Baptist. I should just as strongly object to a Protestant fraternity, although I am a Protestant, or to a Republican fraternity, although I am a Republican.
>
> ". . . Some of the fraternities undoubtedly have clauses in their constitutions which prevent the admission of any but white Protestants. I trust such narrowness will soon be outgrown.
>
> ". . . I believe at Brown we are in advance of many other institutions as is seen by the fact to which you allude—that our football captain is a Jewish young man who has the friendship and loyal support

> of all our students. It is obvious that in our Brown democracy a Jewish student may become a leader recognized and esteemed by all his fellows."

The incident was settled finally by the somewhat technical distinction that Pi Lambda Phi might be admitted, even though none but Jews were members, because there was no clause in its constitution forbidding membership to non-Jews.

Yale is sought out particularly by two classes of Jewish students: the very wealthy and socially ambitious who are attracted by its prestige, and the run-of-mine lad from New Haven's large Jewish population who goes to the university every day to attend classes. The latter group which often does not amalgamate with the student body nor go out exemplifying the Yale polish, presents a difficult problem for "selection". For the university feels itself under certain obligations to the state and city and does not care openly to exclude them. Entrance is primarily by examination, and the Jews amount to ten or fifteen percent of the total.

Questioning Yale men about the treatment of Jewish students, one gathers that in general they associate among themselves and have their own recognized fraternities, that an outstanding Jewish athlete is welcomed, although no Jew was found who had made the crew; publications rather strictly exclude them, the *News* and *Record* staffs being quite on the club basis; in exceptional cases the junior fraternities, Delta Kappa Epsilon and the others, have taken them.

Did you ever hear of a Jew being tapped for the honorary societies: Skull and Bones, Scroll and Keys, Wolf's Head, and the Elihu Club?

"Elihu Club, yes," answered several Yale men. "We've known of one or two. Maybe Wolf's Head. Bones? Never heard of it, and don't think you ever will!"

Chapter V

PROFESSIONAL PREJUDICE

"THE only profession I know of that does not bar Jews is the rabbinical profession," according to Dr. Stephen S. Wise.

But some are more restrictive than others. Medicine is far harder to enter than law. Engineering is unpromising. Teaching is exclusive both in elementary and advanced classifications; in some subjects there is virtually a complete ban against Jewish instructors while others are more liberal.

Nevertheless a traditional respect for learning and a longing for betterment of social position is driving Jews toward professions in disproportionately large numbers. Thousands of young Jews would rather attain standing in a profession than have business success. Prospective fathers-in-law in orthodox Jewish circles even today sometimes pay over their daughter's dowry in advance to assist a young suitor through college.

It has come about, therefore, that more than half the members of the bar in New York City are Jews, and thirty-five percent of the physicians.

Institutes of embalming, barber colleges, and chiropodists' schools feel no problem here, but classes preparing for professions which, *per se,* confer a certain prestige and satisfaction to ambition, find themselves overrun with Jewish applicants. Look upstairs over Foley's undertaking parlors in almost any crowded part of New York and one is likely to see a card identifying the office of Dr. Goldberg, physician and surgeon. If it were Dr. Foley upstairs and Undertaker Goldberg below—that would be news. Jews, in short, have a definite bent beyond other racial groups toward the professions, and naturally they will have a representation more than their strict mathematical proportion of about thirty percent in New York City, and three or four percent of the entire population of the United States.

* * *

The medical colleges look upon this energetic onrushing mass with horror. The plain fact is that if there were not discrimination in the medical colleges of New York City and in other large and famous schools of the East, they would be quite dominated by Jewish students. Considering the great majority of Jewish applicants and their proven ability to learn and to pass examinations, one might estimate readily that selection on a fair scholarship basis would give the medical schools a student body of six or seven Jews out of ten. As discrimination in the centers of Jewish population turns applicants to the West and South, barricades there are thrown up hurriedly.

Even the medical colleges established for Negroes receive applications from Jewish students as a sort of last port in the storm, and they reject them. The medical department of Howard University at Washington, D. C., while accepting one or two Jews every year, declines a much larger number, making the reasonable but final reply:

> "We have felt ourselves obliged to admit a maximum number of colored students to our freshman medical class and a minimum number of representatives from other groups. Just now there is no place in this freshman class which we may offer you."

And Meharry Medical College in Nashville, Tenn., in a state which prohibits by law any mixture in schools of the black and white races, reports that every year from fifteen to twenty-five Jewish students apply.

Yet the question of discrimination against Jews in medicine is the most delicate and difficult chapter in the whole story of prejudice in America. There is less frankness here, more cross currents and division of opinion, greater danger that an intrusion of comment may bring down the wrath alike of those who discriminate and those discriminated against. And there is such need for understanding and courage as to make it most unlikely that written pages can do any good whatever. It is a major problem in diplomacy, still unsettled. In this study are to be presented some of the agenda for an inter-racial conference of conciliation. But the term of the settlement will have to be negotiated delicately by statesmen immediately concerned.

It would be going much too far to ascribe a belligerent hatred to the medical colleges. They are honestly disturbed by what they consider menacing conditions. They greatly desire a solution which they can believe in, and which will not outrage their sense of justice. Even now they are experimenting with "aptitude tests" which may operate only as another bar in the hurdle against Jews but which also may prove a means toward fairer selections.

Certain leading Jewish physicians, proud of their own great men in medicine, devoted to their profession, unwilling to be thought of as complainers, have issued statements denying that there is unfair exclusion. They admit that the Jewish applicant to a medical school in New York has only two-thirds as much chance of acceptance as anybody else—certainly a paragon of restrained statement. But they see this as the result of circumstances and in the eventual best interest of the profession. In the fall of 1930 both *The American Hebrew* and *The*

Jewish Tribune printed long articles, not assuming editorial responsibility for the views expressed, in which successful Jewish practitioners asserted that there was no prejudice or sound basis for criticism, but that the colleges were making a conscientious selection of the most promising applicants. The natural outcry of contradiction was forthcoming immediately.

But there is ample evidence that exclusion is practiced. It is done not only with regret but with good manners, and it is almost never admitted. The colleges do not recognize prejudice as even a bowing acquaintance when they meet on the street. They do not take so much cognizance of discrimination as to attempt to justify it. With few exceptions, their policy is silence.

Poland and Roumania, by contrast, are perfectly candid. They proposed a picturesque form of limitation recently when they said Jewish students would be admitted in proportion to the number of cadavers for dissection supplied by the Jewish communities. Our colleges would blush at such crudeness. But the Jewish student who may be an athlete and popular in undergraduate activities, a youth of proven personal fitness, who presents grades of eighty-five and ninety with his application for admission, is apt to see himself passed over politely, while a Gentile classmate coming from his pre-medical course with grades of seventy-five and eighty is unquestioningly welcomed.

Frankness is rare in exclusions and discriminations, but it is an outstanding virtue in this letter from the registrar of Loyola University in Chicago which tells a Jewish applicant bluntly:

> "I am sorry to have to inform you that your application for admission to the School of Medicine cannot be acted on favorably because the quota for Jewish students has been filled."

And here is the experience of a young Jew in New York City where the motives are less plainly revealed, but in which the implication seems to be much the same. A recent graduate of Columbia College, a Phi Beta Kappa, he applied for admission to the University's College of Physicians and Surgeons. His college record was one A plus, thirteen A's, five A minuses, one B plus, two B's, four B minuses and six C's. Three of the C's were for gymnasium work. One may discount his account as prejudiced testimony, but the fact remains that he was rejected, and the story is this:

> "In February I received a form letter stating that they could not accept my application for admission, but giving no rea-

son for this rejection. At the time they admitted ten Jews and twenty Gentiles from about an equal number of each group applying. Some of the Gentiles had the worst possible grades and unfavorable reports from the committee.

"I then went to two professors for the necessary letters of recommendation to Yale and Harvard. I had been so certain that I would be admitted to P. and S. that I had neglected to apply to the other schools. One professor who is on the faculty committee told me that the members had unanimously favored me and was surprised at my rejection. The committee is composed of the professors of inorganic and organic chemistry, general zoology and physics as well as laboratory assistants. This committee passes on all applicants from Columbia College to P. and S. and reports on each applicant. P. and S. calls this faculty report the best single guide they have for admission.

"The professor also advised me to see the secretary again in order to find out tactfully just why I had been refused and to make sure there had been no mistake.

"I did see him again, and he told me that rejection did not mean that P. and S.

believed the fellow would not make a good doctor or that he was unfit for the study of medicine. He furthermore said that they did not admit all those whom the committee recommended, which is true, but which did not answer why I, in particular, with my good marks and a favorable report, had been rejected.

"He then said the committee had advised their office not to admit all the best Columbia students in order to give other medical schools a chance to get a representative group of Columbia students, whereas otherwise they would get only those who could not get into P. and S. That was empty consolation to me, and furthermore, I did not believe it."

* * *

Assuming in advance of further evidence that discrimination really is practiced, let us take a look at the best face that is put upon it and examine some of the remedies proposed.

The medical profession traditionally is a fraternity, bound by oath, with certain privileges and obligations. And so the fraternity, venerating its past, selects and ordains what successors it wishes, the neophytes entering by act of grace and not of right. Doctors enjoy warming themselves by this distinction, but it is not of great practical influence in keeping out Jews.

Growing out of this tradition somewhat is the loose *sub rosa* slander that Jews are wrecking the profession's ethical standards. It may as well be said in broad daylight that, according to this oft-whispered charge, when Jewish physicians become so numerous that they cannot earn a living legitimately, they exploit their patients, split fees, and specialize in abortion. Beyond any doubt, many a doctor has engaged in malpractice, from economic pressure or perhaps of a free choice. Jews have done so. Gentiles have done so. Are Jews more likely to do so than Gentiles? This seems to be the logical conclusion of the argument, and it would furnish the highest moral ground for exclusion if any school cares to assert it. None, of course, has the courage, or the specific information, to announce such a challenge to the morals of a race. On the other hand it is just as logical to say that when Jews become so numerous that they cannot earn a living in medicine by ethical practice, they voluntarily will go into other occupations.

The trump card of prejudice is an insistence upon holding down Jewish students to a proportionate selection from the whole population. This spirit opens up all the old chasms between separate groups, rather than reaching toward a unity of nation and humanity. On a percentage basis, it can be shown that Jewish students are getting their share. One of the Jewish physicians who wrote denying discrimination cited the figure that seventeen percent of all the medical students in the country are Jewish. Since none but the most famous or most unusually situated Jewish physician, so runs the argument, can hope for any considerable practice outside his own people, why let them increase in numbers? Well, why not let them decide for themselves? Or why not say frankly, we are prejudiced and just won't have them? Or why not adopt the Mussolini system and openly regulate everybody from the top?

Justifications of exclusion and limitation are based entirely upon an acceptance of arbitrary dicta as to what is best for somebody else; not self-determination but submission. The decree from outside saying what the individual may do is the very root of the evil. Even if the results seemed good, it would be bad.

You will remember that at the appearance of *Endymion* by that onetime medical student, John Keats, the wise men and old ones in authority were madly antagonistic, assured that the author was hopelessly wrong, and one critic threw him out in these words:

"So back to the shop, Mr. John, back to plasters, pills and ointment boxes."

If they were fallible in sending John Keats back to be a surgeon's apprentice, what of the cocksure deans today who are sending medical students back to be poets or pawnbrokers, or whatever they may? One wonders to whose gracious permission we are indebted that Abraham Jacoby and Simon Flexner years ago were admitted to medical college. To the good fortune of the English race, the critics had no authority to forbid the poet to write. But the deans can absolutely block a medical career, and there is no getting around them.

So one concludes that the principal remedy for discrimination in medicine is for the medical colleges to drop their prejudice; and on the other hand for the public, and specifically the Jewish community which is most concerned, to make it easier for them to drop it.

States which have their own university medical schools, tax supported, open on necessarily equal terms to all residents, have greatly reduced the hurt of prejudice. For their local Jewish applicants, discrimination as to entrance is slight or actually nonexistent. The Jews' pride may be insulted at times, but opportunity is free.

New York, with more Jewish taxpayers than any other city or state, has no such school. Jewish applicants, if they remain at home, must knock at the door of the city's five principal medical colleges which were founded by Gentiles and are maintained by private contributions. Some of the contributors, of course, have been Jews. If these schools discriminate, there is no recourse; and if they choose to remain preponderantly Gentile in atmosphere, they are but adhering to well-established tradition.

One help certainly would be the establishment of a medical college under the control of Jews. Certain Jews oppose it on the ground that they do not want a medical Ghetto any more than a residential Ghetto. A tax-supported medical school might be formed alongside the College of the City of New York. Long Island University, which is distinct from Long Island Hospital Medical College, has proposed the organization of another medical school—provided support is given. Other projects are being discussed. Wealthy Jews already are predicting that some such school will be equipped and in operation within five years.

Jewish hospitals have existed for years, of course, and advanced education already is being carried on at Mt. Sinai, Beth Israel, the Jewish Hospital in Brooklyn, United Israel, Zion, Montefiore, and others.

And as one more aid to eliminating this constant and painful friction over medical school admissions, instead of compulsion why not try persuasion? Medicine may have become an unfavorable and overcrowded field. Maybe the Jews have overreached themselves. If so, Jewish youngsters ought to be told. The families could direct their interests elsewhere. But when a boy knows in his heart that he wants to be a physician and knows he will pay the price in effort and character and never be satisfied with anything else, no dean or committee on admissions should have the power to tell him No.

* * *

The pressure of Jews trying to get into medical college gets stronger every year, it is complained.

Yes, and the number actually getting in is lower every year. New York Homeopathic Medical College and Flower Hospital, which used to have more Jewish students than any other medical college in the city, is weeding them out. For the year 1929-30, out of a total of 356 students, 245 were Jewish, or 69.1 percent. The graduating class that year consisted of 65 Jews and 18 Gentiles. The same year the college increased its rating from Grade B to Grade A and, apparently, decided that it should do something about having too many Jews. For, whereas the class of 1932 has a membership of 70 Jews and 18 Gentiles, the very next class, 1933, has only 54 Jews and 47 Gentiles. And the class of 1934 has 35 Jews and 69 Gentiles.

Cornell University Medical College, accepting about 65 new students every year, has been cutting down on Jewish admissions also. Of the senior class of 1931, there are 21 Jewish students out of 68 members. The other classes grade off as follows, junior, 13 Jews; sophomore, 9; freshmen, 6.

Long Island Hospital College in Brooklyn admits

about 120 applicants every year. "The percentage of Jewish students has declined markedly in the last three years," a recent investigator reported. "Of the class entered in 1926, nearly 80 percent were Jewish; the class entered in 1927 was not more than 60 percent; the class entered in 1928 was not more than 45 percent."

As to the present Jewish representation in the two other medical colleges: Dean William Darrach of the College of Physicians and Surgeons reported that "Each year we have between 700 and 900 applications. . . . I can state that for the last five years the percentage of Jews in our classes has been pretty close to 20 percent." The college admits about 100 new students every year. The University and Bellevue Hospital Medical College, a branch of New York University, says in its catalogue, "It is proposed to choose 125 of the most promising applicants" every year. It has as many applications every year as Columbia, or more, and the registrar of the university reported that for 1929-30 the Jews were 69.7 percent of the total. This figure probably is the largest of any medical college in the United States, just as N. Y. U. is the most highly Jewish university having a medical department.

All the medical colleges in the city raise the definite issue of whether the applicant is Jewish or not. Whenever the prospective student is a resident of the city, a personal interview is required. A passport photograph must be filed with the application for admission.

Physicians and Surgeons fires in rapid succession "Race?" "Religion?" and "Nationality?" Flower Hospital asks "Religion?" "Naturalized Citizen?" and "Birthplace of Parents?" Cornell asks "What is your racial lineage?"

Cornell has the distinctive rule that "The number of students in this medical college having been limited that its advantages may be equalized to all parts of the state and country, not more than five students from any one college will be admitted to the first year class." An exception, naturally, is made in favor of applicants from Cornell. This rule affords a graceful but definite exclusion of applicants from the strongly Jewish neighboring institutions, N. Y. U. and C. C. N. Y.

* * *

This machinery for exclusion has been grinding steadily, it appears from the figures on entering classes, although with varying severity. Still quite a number of Jews seem to get in. What may the individual expect? What are the odds?

Remember that Long Island College Hospital is one of the schools with a higher proportion of Jews. It is among the more favorable. In the spring of 1929 it happened that a group of one hundred and sixty-three recommended pre-medical students from the College of the City of New York applied for admission to Long Island. The group consisted of one hundred and fifty-one Jews and twelve non-Jews. Only two of all those Jews were accepted; one hundred and forty-nine rejected. But of the non-Jews, five were accepted and seven rejected. It must be added in fairness that the following year, 1930, out of seven City College applicants accepted by Long Island, six were Jews.

If the sweeping exclusion of Jewish applicants is extreme, it also is very frequent. It suggests that either the Jewish students are wretched scholars compared with their extremely desirable classmates, or else some special disqualification works against them. Such experiences have led to the problem of "multiple applications", at present the nightmare of registrars' clerks and admissions committees all over the land.

Students who do not consider themselves sure of getting into the first medical school they apply to have taken up the practice of sending applications to several different colleges at the same time. They hope out of a larger number of possibilities to get in somewhere. There are more than twice the number of applications as of applicants. And nearly half of all those who apply are rejected. In round numbers, for the fall of 1929 there were thirty-one thousand applications, thirteen thousand applicants and seven thousand acceptances.

Jewish students have been the leaders in developing this system. It is a direct outgrowth of the exclusion policy which has created in reality a new young Wandering Jew. Out of the strongly Jewish pre-medical group at the College of the City of New York in 1928, only six felt safe in filing but a single application; thirty-nine filed more than ten each. The Association of American Medical Colleges reported that in 1929 one distrustful student applied to forty-five different institutions.

Dean Burton D. Myers of Indiana University School of Medicine took a typical cross-section group of one hundred and seventy-one multiple applicants and discovered that seventy percent came from within a radius of twenty-five miles of the strongly Jewish and Jew-rejecting City of New York.

The practice is nothing less than a nuisance to the colleges. Something needs to be done about it. And the remedy proposed is to increase the application fees to a prohibitive sum, such as $100. It has not yet been placed in effect, but if it should be, could anyone deny its operation most heavily against Jews?

Investigating the question of whether applicants generally were kept out because of poor grades, the Rev. Dr. Alphonse M. Schwitalla, Jesuit dean of the St. Louis University School of Medicine, charged before the 1929 convention of the association that "selection of freshmen in our schools of medicine is based on other factors than scholarship alone." Admittedly, it is based also upon personality and fitness. Furthermore, it appears strongly to be based upon prejudice against Jews.

Dean Schwitalla reported a student accepted at St. Louis after having been rejected by eighteen other schools, "whose scholarship achievement places him just short of the upper one-fifth of his class." And he concluded, "the scholarship in the school of medicine of the multi-applicant differs, as far as we have been able to discover, in no essential manner from the scholarship of the uni-applicant." Other deans reported similar conclusions.

Glancing at the field outside New York, one discovers the other American medical colleges have about the same proportion of Jews as found within the metropolis, or often a smaller proportion. The Harvard Medical School has a Jewish representation of about nine percent, Yale nineteen and one-half percent, Johns Hopkins between ten and fifteen percent.

The outstandingly famous school of Johns Hopkins seems, indeed, to be about like all the others in this respect. It admits seventy-five new students every year, and the requirement for inclusion of a photograph is underscored on the application blank. The neighboring medical school of the University of Maryland is more liberal with respect to Jews, who account for nearly half its student body. A cautious and impartial informant in Baltimore, commenting upon conditions at Johns Hopkins, wrote:

> "Hopkins is not particularly anxious to have either Jews or women as students, and both groups are therefore restricted. There is nothing official in this, however; that is, there is no official ruling or policy. Under the guidance of the powers that be, the number of Jews is restricted in practice to the percentage I have given. There is no discrimination with respect to Jews as internes at Hopkins or at the University of Maryland. They are the only two hospitals about which I have been able to secure information."

The College of the City of New York is probably the best institution in the United States to approach for data on discrimination against candidates for medical colleges. The Jewish enrollment sometimes reaches as high as ninety percent, and that ratio is fully sustained in the pre-medical group.

Summarizing the experience of applicants from the College of the City of New York for several years past, the conclusions are that:

Only a limited number of its students get into medical colleges.

The proportion is getting smaller every year.

The Jews from the college fare much worse than the non-Jews.

Turning toward the United States as a whole, the same conclusion as to exclusion of Jews is reached, even though the evidence is less violently outstanding than in what might be called the test tube conditions of New York City.

State university medical schools are coming to a policy of excluding non-resident applicants; and of course this is a perfectly natural tendency of self-protection against groups from far away who, by the very weight of numbers, may wear out their welcome.

In consequence of rejections all over their own country, Jewish medical students are to be found in dozens of foreign universities, as far as half way around the world.

So much for assertion and conclusions. The figures are forthcoming.

* * *

About half of those admitted to New York University's department, the University and Bellevue Hospital Medical College, are themselves N. Y. U. men. This takes care to a considerable extent of the high percentage of Jewish pre-medical students in one of the city's institutions. Columbia has a percentage of Jews in its medical school nearly as high as in the college. But the College of the City of New York has no medical department. Its prospective physicians must go outside for their education. The figures quoted here as to the reception they meet are drawn almost entirely from the official records of the college.

The exact comparison of relative success of Jewish and non-Jewish applicants from the College of the City of New York for all medical schools, not just those in the city, during four years is as follows:

	Number of applicants	*Number accepted*	*Percentage of group accepted*
1927			
Non-Jewish	15	12	80 %
Jewish	183	91	49.7%
1928			
Non-Jewish	16	11	68.7%
Jewish	185	73	39.4%
1929			
Non-Jewish	16	12	75 %
Jewish	222	58	26.1%
1930			
Non-Jewish	19	14	73.7%
Jewish	280	55	19.7%

In 1929 there were 553 applications from City College students to the five medical colleges in the city, and 42 acceptances or 7.5 percent, as follows:

	Applications	*Acceptances*
Columbia P. and S.	43	1
Cornell	62	3
Bellevue	170	15
Long Island	163	7
Flower	115	16

The foregoing refers to applications. A great many City College students are multiple applicants. In 1930 the number of applicants accepted from the college, by the New York City schools, was forty-one and their distribution was almost exactly the same, suggesting almost a fixed allotment.

Considering medical schools throughout the United States and Canada as a whole, one observes that the percentage of acceptances from the strongly Jewish College of the City of New York is noticeably lower than for the average from all the pre-medical schools. Here is the table:—

	Percentage of all applicants accepted by 80 medical colleges	*Percentage of CCNY applicants accepted*
1926	75.6	57.2
1927	57.6	53.2
1928	55.5	41.8

Viewing the City College picture for the year 1930, it appears that 299 students applied for admission to American medical schools and 69 were accepted, or 23.1 percent. In addition to the 41 already credited to the five local medical schools, there were 28 placed in schools outside the city, as follows:—

Boston University	1	Michigan	1
Creighton	7	Mississippi	1
Georgetown	1	Pennsylvania	1
Howard	2	St. Louis	1
Loyola	2	Texas	1
Maryland	7	Washington (St. Louis)	1
McGill	1	Western Ontario	1

The percentage of success of City College applicants is increased somewhat by the addition of its thirty-nine applicants who entered foreign medical colleges, or thirteen percent of those who applied abroad. These are located as follows:—

Berlin	10	Lausanne	1
Berne	1	London	5
Bologna	1	Paris	1
Bonn	1	St. Andrews	3
Edinburgh	1	Vienna	7
Geneva	1	Zurich	4
Glasgow	3		

* * *

One of the most complete sets of data yet attempted concerning racial representation in medical colleges was the result of a questionnaire sent out in the spring of 1930 by Dr. A. J. Rongy, the eminent Jewish gynecologist in New York, who is one of those, by the way, who has written to defend the colleges from the charge of unfairness. This material he kindly placed at the disposal of the authors of this book. The table which follows, compiled from his facts, concerns thirty-one medical colleges outside of New York City, scattered all over the United States, including some of the most famous schools, and accounting for approximately 40 percent of them all. It is presented here as a contribution to the understanding of the whole problem.

The table follows:—

	Total enroll-ment	*Jews*
Baylor University College of Medicine	345	14
Boston University School of Medicine	413	200
University of Chicago, Rush Medical College.	305	75
University of Cincinnati College of Medicine.	245	46
Creighton School of Medicine	240	18
University of Georgia Medical Department.	139	14
George Washington University Medical School.	290	79
Hahneman Medical College, Philadelphia.	455	49
Harvard University Medical School	510	46
University of Illinois College of Medicine.	575	198

	Total	*Jews*
Indiana University	420	24
Jefferson Medical College, Philadelphia	592	116
University of Louisville, Medical Department	350	52
University of Kansas School of Medicine	233	16
Marquette University Medical School	345	44
University of Maryland School of Medicine	413	200
University of Michigan Medical School	636	88
Ohio State, College of Medicine	324	48
University of Oklahoma Medical School	200	4
University of Pennsylvania Medical School	469	70
University of Pittsburgh Medical School	260	30
University of Southern California College of Medicine (first and second year classes only)	92	16
University of Syracuse Medical School	182	40
Temple University, Philadelphia	290	95
University of Tennessee College of Medicine	405	23
University of Texas Medical School	310	10
University of Toronto Medical School	725	115
Tufts College Medical School	486	189

	Total	Jews
Western Reserve, Medical School...	241	41
University of Virginia Medical School	245	16
Yale University School of Medicine ..	215	42
Total......................	10,950	2,018

These figures show a Jewish representation in the colleges named, outside of New York, of 18 4/10 percent. That is not far from the estimate for the whole country, already quoted, of 17 percent of the medical students being Jewish. It indicates that these institutions are fairly representative, or a shade more generous than the average toward Jews.

* * *

Comment from students and teachers concerning local conditions reflected in the foregoing tables in some cases is enlightening.

One of the nine Jewish students at the University of Texas Medical School wrote a letter saying, loyally, "Not the slightest trace of anti-semitism exists on our campus."

But a Jewish student at the University of Iowa said:

> "Out-of-state students are no longer allowed to enter the school of medicine, and as practically all out-of-state students of medicine are Jews from the eastern states,

> it directly affects them. Eastern Jews have not been very popular in the school of medicine. Probably just a conflict of cultures."

Several of the deans wrote frankly concerning their difficulties, of which the following are illuminating examples.

From Creighton University School of Medicine, Omaha, Neb.:

> "Our policy is to admit ten percent of Jewish students. As this is a Catholic institution entirely dependent financially on Catholic support, we feel justified in this practice, especially as our applications from Jewish students of this state and its vicinity fall far below the permitted percentage."

From the University of Alabama School of Medicine:

> "If we should accept all the Jewish applicants from the Northeast who offer three or four years of preparation and whose references as to character, etc., seem satisfactory, we should fill up our freshman class twice over and exclude all our own native sons. Obviously this would be un-

> just to the people who support the state university."

From West Virginia University School of Medicine:

> "Of the students making application, the greater number come from New York. I would say that about ninety percent are Jewish and the others are practically all Italians. When we first had to limit the number of students we could accept, there were very few of these students coming here for their premedical work, but in order to increase the possibilities of getting in our school, they began to take their premedical work here, so much so that the majority of our premedical class are Jewish students from New York and the vicinity.
>
> "Some of these men we have accepted into our classes, but if we accepted all who apply, we could fill our school ten times over with Jewish students. I would judge this is the condition everywhere. We have never refused to accept a Jewish student whose home is in West Virginia. I have had these West Virginia Jews say that they disliked very much the Jewish students

from New York City, because of their aggressiveness and their feeling of superiority, their display and making themselves so conspicuous.

"We make no discrimination between Protestants and Catholics *per se,* so that no one's religion enters into the matter.

"Last year we reported nine hundred and one students making application for admission to our school, who met our requirements for entrance, and that did not include the number who made application but failed to meet our requirements, because we were too short of help to follow up the correspondence with them further than to inform them we had no vacancies. I think I would be safe in saying that of these nine hundred and one mentioned, at least six hundred were Jewish."

Exclusion from medicine in the United States has driven Jewish students to far-away and foreign schools. As already noted, City College reported thirty-seven students placed abroad in 1929. The same year, six hundred Americans, almost all Jews, applied at Edinburgh, and about thirty were admitted.

A student in St. Andrews at Dundee in 1928 wrote back: "There are seventeen Americans in the second year here. All are Jewish with the exception of one who is a Negro." The expense, the difference in methods and associations, the uncertainty of getting hospital appointments later at home—all these factors and perhaps others make it a disadvantage to study medicine abroad. But what can the Jewish student do after he has prepared and been refused at home? He can try to get in—even as far away as Manila or Siam—or he can turn toward dentistry or pharmacy.

* * *

Jewish students who get through medical college find prejudice pursuing them. They encounter quotas or bans upon interneships in the better hospitals. They are shunted into the less desirable medical assignments, and away from surgery. They have difficulty in getting staff appointments except in Jewish hospitals, and if they desire to teach, their opportunities are slight. In the course of professional practice, the Jewish physician meets a quota in entering academies of medicine and medical societies. Every step is cluttered up with arbitrary handicaps from which non-Jewish competitors are free.

A half dozen or so of the larger hospitals in New York, with their great variety of ailments under treatment and their superior equipment, are particularly sought for interneships. Among these, of course, are Mt. Sinai and Beth Israel, which make provision for dozens of Jewish internes. Some hospitals, year after year, do not admit any Jewish internes; others will take one of conspicuous and notable brilliance. One hospital has a quota of two Jewish internes a year, no more. Jewish physicians say of one or two hospitals, "They will take a Jewish interne if his father is very wealthy." At Bellevue there are four divisions of internes, one of which is open, the other three being controlled as a vested interest by the Columbia, Cornell, and N. Y. U. medical colleges respectively. Such divisions have the effect of maintaining quotas and arbitrary representation.

The sort of experience which makes Jews believe that discrimination is no myth was told by a college professor, concerning one of his former students. He said:

> "He was doing unusually well and was invited to carry on some special research under a leading authority on nutrition in America. Early in his senior year the student was advised by this professor not to make application to any of the hospitals for an interneship nor to take any of the qualifying examinations, because the medical school and specifically the professor had the naming of a certain number of graduates who were to serve as internes in one

of the hospitals now part of the medical center uptown.

"The young man was naturally overjoyed. He came to me with the story, but I urged him to make every effort to get into Mt. Sinai. Much against his will, he took the examination and made a very high place on the Mt. Sinai list. He was sent for by the superintendent of the hospital to which this professor had recommended him and was received rather coldly.

"Two days later his professor sent for him, was most profuse in his apologies, accepted the blame for having misled the student, unwittingly to be sure, and told the young man that those of his origin were not accepted by the hospital in question. He did not know the young man's origin and furthermore he did not care, but the hospital was adamant.

"He said he hardly knew what to do to help the young man get into a hospital now that the examination time was passed. The young man explained that he had been urged by a friend to take the Mt. Sinai examinations and had made the list. This news was a great relief to the professor who, I am sure, is absolutely honest in all his professions.

"The young man, after serving his interneship, was chosen for a post-graduate scholarship by his medical school and studied abroad under a liberal financial allowance an entire year. He has made good in his chosen profession and in his specialty. The number of older and experienced men who sent patients to this young man may be regarded as evidence for my statement that he has made good."

The famous Kings County Hospital case in Brooklyn in June, 1927, probably is the most extreme recent incident of mistreatment of Jewish internes. There were four on the staff, and on the night in question, one happened to be absent. In the middle of the night about twenty men woke up the three Jews, bound, gagged and ducked them in tubs of ice water and otherwise hazed them.

Charges of race discrimination were made at once, covering alleged mistreatment of Jews for years past. It was said that the first Jewish interne at the hospital, a Dr. Oldstein, had entered eleven years before, but that he had been tied up, taken to the Grand Central Station and sent out of the city on a train with the warning that if he returned, he would be thrown into the river. He did not come back, and there had been no Jewish interne at the hospital until the admission of one of those hazed, Dr. Soloway, about two years before.

The three Jews charged that they had been warned by fellow internes to leave the staff and told, "This is a Christian institution and we will tolerate no Jews here." Among their complaints was that the Jews were not allowed to sit at the same table with non-Jewish doctors but ate at a "kosher" table; they were not allowed to play on the hospital tennis courts although they offered to contribute to their upkeep; they were subject to slurring remarks; nurses were discourteous to them; Jewish patients were neglected, and the Jewish internes were not summoned promptly to patients in urgent need of treatment.

The case provoked three investigations. Six internes in the hospital were identified by the victims. After they made formal apology, the complainants withdrew their charges of assault. Commissioner of Accounts James A. Higgins investigated by order of the mayor, and reported that the charges of discrimination at the hospital were well-founded. The superintendent was suspended but later he made an answer to the charges and was reinstated.

Jewish physicians encounter discrimination, also, in a restriction of hospital facilities. There is definite limitation upon their admission to the staffs of the better non-Jewish hospitals, although staff connections are becoming increasingly essential to effective first-class practice. Staff positions above the grade of interne mount through assignments in the outpatient department, chief of clinic, adjunct physician or surgeon, associate, attending and consulting staff physicians. Those of the grade of adjunct and above may bring their patients to the hospital and treat them there.

If any person is curious as to the small number of Jews admitted, he may obtain convincing data from the green-bound *Medical Directory of New York, New Jersey and Connecticut,* turning to the list of hospital staffs in New York City. The Jewish hospital lists are filled with Jewish-sounding names. On the lists of the leading non-Jewish hospitals there are scarcely any Jewish names in the consulting, attending, or associate classifications.

Among themselves, the hospitals are frank on this point. Friendly executives in the non-Jewish hospitals advise promising young Jewish physicians to go to their own people, "they probably could do more for you." They send recommendations of Jewish chiefs of clinic and adjunct physicians to the Jewish hospitals, recognizing that they can not go far unless they made a change. Some of the hospitals have a rule that no one may become an attending physician unless he is a graduate of the house staff, at the same time enforcing a rule against Jewish internes.

The great medical institution of the Mayo Brothers at Rochester, Minnesota, probably the most famous of the kind in the United States, consists of the Mayo Clinic, a group of physicians conducting a private practice, and the Mayo Foundation, a part of the Graduate School of the University of Minnesota. Answering inquiries concerning Jews there, the director of the foundation courteously reported that in the clinic one Jew is associate head of an important department, one Jew is on the faculty of the Foundation and on the staff of the clinic, and that there are six Jewish Fellows out of two hundred and thirty-seven studying under the Foundation. The director reported: These six were nominated because they were among the best applicants available. The Jewish applicants who were not nominated were refused because they were not among the best."

Speaking of hospitals, there are troubles in wait there also for Jewish girls who wish to become trained nurses. One case of personal acquaintance concerns a pretty Jewish girl who contemplated entering a hospital for training in the fall, and, being out of town, asked a friend to get her some literature and information about the course. The friend went to the Presbyterian Hospital at the Medical Center. The superintendent of nurses asked what was the applicant's name.

"Hurwitz," was the reply. . . . "Oh, then," said the official, "why doesn't she enter one of the Jewish hospitals?" . . . . It was explained that she was interested in the Presbyterian, but wanted to get information from several. "But," said the superintendent, "I am sure she would be happier at a Jewish hospital amongst her own kind." The friend talked and argued, and asked again for literature. She got none, and left.

Medical college professorships are also among the prizes which hang too high for any but a few exceptional Jews. The number of Jewish professors in New York City is small, and decreasing. When a Jewish professor retires or resigns, as a matter of routine he seems to be replaced by a Gentile. And when a Gentile retires or resigns, he likewise is replaced by a Gentile. Out of seventy-three active professors and assistant professors at the Cornell Medical school, there is one Jewish professor and one assistant. Out of forty-one at Bellevue, there is one professor, one associate and two assistants. Out of forty-two at Physicians and Surgeons there are three Jews; and of fifty-four at Flower, four. Outside of New York there are some, including the dean of the Yale Medical School. The field of greatest opportunity for Jews in medical practice apparently is in psychiatry and neurology.

Looking back over this progression of handicaps, it reads like an advertisement for Jewish doctors. If they come through, they must be good.

* * *

So the ambitious young Jew decides not to be a doctor after all. He will become a lawyer.

In preparing for the practice, he will benefit from an economic alliance which is just the reverse of his brother's experience as an aspirant to medicine. Law schools, especially the night schools, usually operate at a profit. The more students, the more income. Medical education is costly, requiring laboratories and clinics which the student's fees cannot pay for, and which make him the favorite of some trust fund or endowment. The law schools on the other hand are prepared to sell him as much education as he has money to buy. Even the day law schools, the best ones in the land, welcome qualified students without objection to religious variations. The night law schools around New York show that about nine out of ten of their students are Jewish. New York University reported for 1929–30 that sixty-seven and nine-tenths percent of its law students were Jews, and Columbia has twice the percentage of Jews in its law school as in medicine.

The law by comparison with medicine appears, in fact, as a land flowing with milk and honey. There is Brandeis on the United States Supreme Court, Mack on the federal Circuit Court of Appeals, and Cardozo, chief justice of the New York State Court of Appeals. There is the eminent Samuel Untermyer and Colonel Joseph M. Hartfield in the great Wall Street firm of White & Case. In Chicago there was the late Levy Mayer, one of the great successes of the bar, and in the less austere activities of the profession, Charles Erbstein is a leader in getting divorces, and Judge Sabath in granting them. Even among young lawyers, consider Henry J. Friendly, who received, after Justice Brandeis, the highest grades ever given at the Harvard Law School, who was much sought after when he came to New York a few years ago and obtained a berth in the desirable firm of Root, Clark, Buckner, Howland and Ballantine.

The young Jewish aspirant to the bar, if he will turn to the Christian Bible, will find a passage which says, "Woe unto you, ye lawyers." But he will not believe it at first.

Let us return to our fictitious Jewish student, Mannie Levy, who had difficulty getting into Columbia College and later went to the University of Pennsylvania or elsewhere. Here he is now, all agog for human justice and legal subtlety.

To his delight he finds that Columbia University, which demands a passport photograph with applications to enter the college or the College of Physicians and Surgeons, has no such requirement for the law school. He will be admitted there, or he may go to Harvard or Yale. He may choose from the most famous law schools in the country. And in the school he will be treated quite fairly. There will be a number of Jewish professors and instructors. He may share a dormitory room or suite with a Gentile classmate. The whole atmosphere is rather fraternal. He will get a chance purely on merit for a place on the cherished Columbia or Harvard *Law Review* or the Yale *Law Journal,* the magazine staff composed of the fifteen men with the highest grades in the class. Often as many as half the *Review* or *Journal* men will be Jews.

Occasionally on the school bulletin board he will see a notice that some law firm has a vacancy for a recent graduate, the typewritten slip being phrased something like this: "Wanted, "A" man of the best oldfashioned stock." This will be notice that no Levys need apply. During the Christmas vacation of his senior year, Mannie Levy will go to New York with most of his classmates, Jewish and Gentile alike, to be interviewed by the big offices with reference to jobs after graduation. And here he will learn at first hand the importance of being Gentile.

The Harvard Law School Joint Committee on Employment in New York each year sends to the senior class a list of firms that wish to interview young lawyers with reference to employment. Some of the firm names are marked with a star, indicating an interest only in "A" and "B" grade men. Others are marked with two stars; they say they "wish to interview Gentiles." On one of the most recent lists, only three firms marked themselves with two stars: —Gould and Wilkie; Kirlin, Woolsey, Campbell, Hickox and Keating; and Loomis Ruebush, all in the financial district. Many firms have not such candor, and although they will see Jewish applicants, they never offer a position.

Looking at New York now through the hopeful eyes of our young lawyer, Mannie Levy, let us inquire what chance he has to find employment. The question was put to several experienced lawyers who had spent time aiding Jewish graduates.

"Ninety percent of the big firms won't take a Jew under any circumstances," was the answer.

Now, frankly, that estimate probably is too pessimistic, taken literally. Glance over the best firms in the city and you will find quite a sprinkling of Jewish lawyers. Among the big firms, certainly it is not true that ninety percent at present do not have any Jewish lawyers on their staffs. They have. The famous firm of Hughes, Schurman and Dwight for a period of five years or more had just one Jew on its staff. The firm of which Elihu Root and Emory R. Buckner are members is widely known as one of the most liberal toward Jews, having several on its staff, including a partner. But if one considers the vacancies open to young graduates, it is perfectly accurate to say that ninety percent are not open to Jews.

The handicap of race appears in two ways. It is more difficult for a Jewish lawyer to get a start. And it is excessively difficult if he is only slightly better than average. There are Jews who, by means of unusual social connections or by "getting the breaks" in other ways, may happen to enter offices closed to every other Jew but themselves, and they may even become members of their firms. The youngster who seems to have the potentialities of a Justice Brandeis will get along. But the "B" grader will be pushed aside ruthlessly in favor of the "B" grade Gentile. The extraordinary individual case, however, is of no help to our Jewish lad with no brilliant special qualifications or outside support, who is just looking for a chance to pitch in with a will and do the hard work of law practice.

Mannie Levy looks over the New York field, and this is what he sees:

Upon one side are the old, long-established firms which conduct the affairs of the great corporations, banks and wealthy estates of the country, the "top ring" which represents one client or the other in virtually all the big deals of national business. On the other side are offices handling general practice, personal representation, real estate, criminal, divorce, political and miscellaneous legal matters, shading down to ambulance chasing and fixing it up in a magistrate's court, the practice which can be conducted independently and which includes thousands of unknown and fiercely competitive individual practitioners. In the first order are such firms as Cravath, DeGersdorff, Swaine and Wood; Cadwalader, Wickersham and Taft; Davis, Polk, Wardwell, Gardiner and Reed; Murray, Aldrich and Webb, and so on. Such great organizations are inclined to wonder even that one of their members would withdraw to become a candidate for governor or to accept an appointment to the President's cabinet. There is an amazing concentration of the wealth, prestige and influence of the whole profession in a comparatively small group of downtown New York law firms. Their recruits are drawn almost exclusively from the more famous law schools of the Atlantic coast, with an occasional opening for men from Cornell, Northwestern, and the better-known inland schools. Positions in these offices are prizes. Law offices grade off from these in varying importance, many of them affording excellent if secondary opportunities to young graduates, many more having practically nothing at all to offer, some few among them taking graduates from the night schools.

Most of the great firms leading in corporation practice are traditionally Gentile. They have gone along for decades and generations with Gentile personnel—since long before the city acquired its tremendous Jewish population—strengthening associations with old clients, growing in familiarity with corporation law, adding new business connections as new companies developed. They amount, really, to a privileged and aristocratic guild within their own profession. A few Jewish firms come within this group, such firms as Guggenheimer, Untermyer and

Marshall; Cook, Nathan and Lehman; Hays, Herschfield and Wolf, and a limited number of others. No invidious comparison is intended toward either Jewish or Gentile firms mentioned or omitted. The names used are simply types. But where such Jewish firms could be counted on your fingers, the corresponding Gentile establishments are found by scores. Jewish firms naturally are subjected to extreme pressure to take law graduates of their own race, and often there are enough rising lawyers in the partners' own families to fill the vacancies. And so arises the surplus of young Jewish lawyers.

Offices seeking young lawyers for junior positions are guided to a great extent by the grades received in school. Among the very most favored are men from the Harvard and Columbia *Reviews* and the Yale *Law Journal.* These forty-five young lawyers each year, representing the equivalent of Phi Beta Kappa in three of the most respected law schools, are pointed, everything being equal, toward the highest places.

But everything is not equal. Of recent years, Jewish students have been entering the law in larger numbers, and with their keen minds, ambition and knack for passing examinations, they have proved their ability to get excellent grades. Often from the three schools, twenty of these honor men are Jews and twenty-five non-Jews; or even vice versa. Under present conditions, nothing but their own latent deficiencies can stop these Gentile honor graduates. By Christmas of their senior year, they have arranged for places in their own choices from the leading firms in New York. So great is the demand for them that about 1927 the leading firms in self defense agreed upon a maximum salary of two hundred dollars a month for these beginners, in order to stop excessive bidding into which they were being forced.

But the price for Jews of Law Review class is not run up by mad bidding. Twenty or twenty-five of them longingly knock at the doors of the big offices every year. Ten or a dozen are chosen by the larger Jewish firms; three or four perhaps by the Gentile firms. What can the others do? First class brains, cursed by excessive standards acquired in superior schools, find themselves going to waste. What can they do? About three choices are open: they may take what jobs they can get, often in second-rate offices, at from nothing to fifteen dollars a week, accepting greatly reduced chances for eventual success; or a few of them may take research jobs around the law schools or with surveys and social service foundations which do not recognize racial handicaps; or, in the third place, they may give up their profession and enter business. The difficulty is all the greater for Jewish graduates of lesser attainment, the men who got grades of "B" and "C."

Discrimination emphatically does exist in the practice of law in New York. Dozens of firms talking over the telephone with the employment secretary or volunteer alumnus committeeman of the law school, will say:

"Just any good man of high scholarship and suitable personality. Oh no, there's no religious prejudice here. Any good man. Of course, no Jews!"

Why is this?

Habit, for one reason. The firms never have employed Jews. Inertia says they never will. Why change?

The clients, for another reason. Many estates and corporations—or so the law firms believe—do not wish to deal with Jewish lawyers.

Still another reason is a feeling that admitting one Jewish lawyer is an entering wedge, and the firm does not desire gradually to become known as Jewish. So it has come about that some of the largest Jewish financial houses are represented by firms which do not employ Jewish lawyers at all. The firms consider such exclusion a necessary act of self-defense. For their Jewish clients frequently would ask the placement of a son or nephew recently graduated from a good law school. If the firm says bluntly that it is its policy to take no Jews at all—regardless of family or personal desirability—it has come to be accepted as a proper and satisfactory reply.

There is the reason, also, that firms wish their staff and new partners to bring in clients. This is especially true among the so-called "polo playing firms". They represent not only the rich but also the more exclusive social groups, wishing their business to develop among these classes. It is highly desirable business, with its prospect of vast estates and trusts to administer. These office rosters read like the social register, and few there be even of the Gentiles who enter therein. Some of the large Jewish firms likewise limit or reject Jews from their staffs, seeking those who can attract Gentile business. This policy of theirs, incidentally, is cited everywhere by prejudiced Gentiles as a taunt and a justification.

The employment office of one large law school, among the most famous in the East, furnishes the statement that during the past three years, more than sixty percent of the positions offered for its law graduates definitely requested Gentiles. The exact items are these: out of four hundred and three positions offered, two hundred and sixty-nine were apparently for Christians only; seventy-six made no specification, and fifty-eight implied that Jews would be preferred. The same office gives figures on the number of graduates registering as applicants for help in obtaining positions. Those who had jobs at graduation naturally did not register, so the figures are significant in their inverse implications. And less than half the members of the class were Jewish. Registrations for the class of 1930 of men without jobs showed fifty-one Gentiles, two unclassified, and seventy Jews. The year before, there were forty-three Gentiles, three unclassified and sixty-four Jews. The process of getting jobs for Jewish lawyers is slower and more difficult.

An agency in New York which offers employment service for professional people reported that in 1930, out of a couple of thousand lawyers registered, more than half of them being Jewish, it placed a total of about one hundred and fifty. Less than two dozen of these were Jewish.

A Jewish graduate of the Fordham University law school, who did not look markedly Jewish, was applying for a place in the legal department of one of the larger banks. Unless he changed his name, he was told, he would not have a chance because the bank would not want to refer a client to any lawyer with a Jewish name. Another in filling out a blank in application for a place in the legal department of an insurance company recorded that his father's religion was Presbyterian, his mother's, Jewish. The company had a policy against employing Jews in any capacity, he was told. True, his was a borderline case, but he could not be taken.

A personal memory goes back through the years to a conversation as a law student in Chicago with a professor in the school. The subject was the increasing stringency of scholarship requirements for taking the bar examinations. Retrospection has strengthened the impression that this professor was far from infallible, although on occasion he has been known to be right. And for whatever they may be worth, his remarks on scholarship requirements were:

> "You know why the bar association is insisting upon higher standards, don't you? It is to keep out the Jews. They're overrunning the profession, and something must be done about it. The trouble is that the Jews are taking these preliminary college years without a hitch, and we're keeping out the Christians instead."

The Association of the Bar of New York has had several Jewish vice-presidents and members of important committees, and prejudice there has not been charged in recent times. However, there is a member of the bar now living, who was, supposedly, excluded from the association because of race prejudice. The incident is mentioned here as an odd relic of fact and also as an example of what can happen. It was referred to by George William Curtis, then editor of Harper's Magazine, in the issue of July, 1877, in these words:

> "Recently in New York an estimable and accomplished gentleman was rejected as a member of the Bar Association 'for no

> reason that can be conceived,' indignantly said one of the leading members, 'except that he was a Jew.' Doubtless few votes would procure the rejection. But the association is not a social club, and presumptively a man who is an honorable member of the bar is a fit member of the association. The few hostile votes, however, represent the prejudice. It is very old and very universal."

* * *

Gentile students outnumber the Jews in just one department at the College of the City of New York: the School of Engineering. Here they number nearly sixty percent. New York University, predominantly Jewish in other departments, finds Jews making up only about one-fourth of its engineering classes. Columbia has a Jewish group of only seven or eight percent of the total enrollment in engineering. This is not because of discrimination in these schools, nor because there is no money to be made in the profession. It probably is because of the advice passed along year after year from mouth to mouth: "Stay out of engineering. They don't like Jews and won't give us a chance." Stupid though such advice may be, how did it come to be given? Is there any reason?

The most conservative answer received in this inquiry was from the manager of a large technical employment service who was not quite an unbiased witness. He had personal associations which made him see himself, perhaps, in the role of defender of his profession from attack or disparagement. He estimated, however, that about one-fourth of the positions open specified that no Jews might be sent; but he thought a Jew with attractive personality might even be employed in most of those. The very big corporations, and the very small ones employing only one or two engineers, were the most difficult, he thought. Yes, some of the big Jewish-owned companies were just as bad as any about refusing Jewish help. There seemed to be more Jews in electrical and chemical engineering, fewer in civil, mechanical and mining. This is one man's opinion.

Another employment specialist rated the influence of prejudice thus: "Take the average, reasonably suitable Gentile applicant for a technical position and grade him eighty percent of ideal requirements. Another man of approximately the same fitness, if he is a Jew, usually must be graded down. In a few cases, he may rate a full eighty, too. But you probably will have to drop him down to forty percent, or even to nothing at all. His race is almost certain to be more or less of a handicap, and at best it is no asset."

In the technical professions even as among the run of low-priced stenographers, race and religion prove a burden. The same engineering corporations and public utility companies which refuse to employ Jewish office workers, are unfriendly to Jewish engineers. So it is not uncommon for these highly-trained men to change their names. A man reported that he received the friendly advice from an agency: "If you persist in saying you are a Jew, you might as well bury yourself right away." The prize story in one agency is about a hardy name-changer who registered three times within a few months, the first time as a Jew, the second as a Catholic, the third as a Protestant. The names given in order were Wallach, Wallack and Wallace.

The manager of the Technical Service Agency in New York has experienced a practical limitation on Jews which held them to the lower-priced positions paying from fifteen dollars a week up to one hundred dollars or at the outside, one hundred and fifty dollars. Some Jewish engineers hold extremely lucrative positions, he admitted, but they obtained them through personal access to their employers and not through an agency. He told of placing Gentiles sometimes in positions paying from fifteen thousand dollars to thirty thousand dollars a year. For the higher positions, he thought, employers who are Jewish themselves, sometimes want Christians, and the Christians nearly always specify "no Jews".

Summarizing opinions of several professionals in technical employment, chemistry is least favorable to Jews and architectural work the most. Yet so inconsistent is the whole problem of prejudice that a Jewish professor now is president of the American Chemical Society.

There is a general surplus of qualified men in chemistry, according to the experts. Therefore, Jews find it "a slough of despond, a sink of iniquity, a pitfall and a snare, the path to heartbreak house."

Take down the electrical and chemical engineering trade papers and look at the classified advertisements of positions needing men. The familiar phrases occur frequently:—"State race and religion," "Applications lacking photographs will be discarded," and "Protestant". Notices of positions wanted reflect the thought that it is worth while to disavow Jewishness in describing one's qualifications. A particularly frank notice was published in January, 1930, in *Industrial and Engineering Chemistry*. It said:

> "PATENT EXPERT, CHEMICAL—Progressive, rapidly-growing chemical corporation requires full time services of patent expert capable of assuming executive responsibilities. Applicants should be from 28 to 35 years old and must have graduated in chemistry or chemical engineering from high-grade school. . . . Legal training not essential but highly desirable. Christians preferred. Address Box 18-N-12."

The larger construction companies seldom employ Jews, say the agencies, while smaller contractors are more favorable. This is explained in that organizations employing hundreds of men seek to regulate everything by general policy, while in smaller groups there is a greater element of personal judgment. At the same time an apparent anti-Jewish policy in a large organization may result entirely from the prejudice of one department chief, while they fare well elsewhere in the concern.

Surveying once offered a fair opportunity for Jews. Of late, title companies have taken it over increasingly, and Jews are being eliminated.

Generalizing again, there is little prejudice in mechanical and industrial work of a technical nature. There is quite a good deal in designing. There are almost no Jewish superintendents of construction on the larger building projects in New York.

Radio, at the beginning, was teeming with Jews. Now some of the larger companies are reported as unfavorable to Jewish engineers. Even in small shops which often are operated by Jews, the repair men—as being in a sense contact men with the public—are sought from among non-Jews.

Considering technical employment geographically, agencies rate New York as the most unfavorable locality in the United States for Jews. New England is virtually the same. Philadelphia is considered easy. The rest of the country is reported more friendly to Jews, increasingly so as one travels away from New York.

* * *

"Is there no way at all that I can get a professorship of Latin in an American college?" exclaimed a perplexed Jewish scholar who had spent years fitting himself for a professional career which apparently never was going to begin.

"Why certainly you may," said another Jew. "Just have Felix Warburg endow a chair for you."

A letter from a discouraged Jewish master of arts from Harvard said,

> "The head of the appointment office for teachers at University Hall has told me plainly that it is almost impossible to place Jewish graduates of Harvard in teaching positions, that the schools and colleges simply won't entertain the idea. It makes no odds how brilliant the Jewish candidate may be."

One of the most distinguished of American historians, who has a long and varied academic background, wrote in answer to an inquiry concerning his observations:

> "Here are some random thoughts on your subject. Prejudice against Jews is not

peculiar to Jews. It runs against other races and all outsiders, barbarians, as the Greeks called them. It is as old as the tribe and exists in all races and nationalities. That much ought to be made clear at the outset.

"Here is an authentic story. A professor in a certain large eastern university needed an assistant. The most brilliant student in his graduate class was a young Jew. The professor proposed this young man for the position, but the head of the institution replied: 'Let us be loyal to our own race.' A Nordic about twenty-five per cent below the Jew in native ability and acquired knowledge got the place.

"In my department no discriminations were made against Jews either as to admission to courses, grades, or advancement. I found by experience that it was very difficult to find places for Jews in American colleges, and frequently advised graduates to go in for law or medicine. Only a few Jews, relatively, are found on the teaching staffs of American colleges. The shining exceptions almost prove the rule. But here religion as well as race enter into consideration. Small denominational colleges usu-

> ally want fairly orthodox teachers of their own persuasion.
>
> "The thing is very complex, and you should be on your guard against ascribing to prejudice an action that might arise from some other motive. Personally, I have been skinned and robbed more often by pure Nordics than by Jews. There is nobody like a pure Yankee for the game of skinning. But Jews sometimes appear worse because they do it with more unction, it seems."

Dr. Edwin R. A. Seligman, professor of political economy and one of the most distinguished members of the Columbia faculty, himself a Jew, recognizes frankly that some colleges do not employ Jewish instructors and says the feeling unquestionably is growing, but:

> "I tell my students that there is no reason why they shouldn't go ahead with their ambitions and ideals," he said in personal conversation. "There is only one point for them to consider; they must be much better than their competitors. As Jews they cannot get anywhere by being only as good.
>
> "There are any number of able young Jews in political science today. It is much

> easier to get a job in research work than in teaching, but even that can be done by the proper personality and effort. One of my Jewish students once committed suicide because of discouragement at not getting placed. But he was impatient. If he had only waited, I could have found a place for him."

The favorite target for complaints of anti-Jewish bias toward teachers around New York is New York University. A recent essayist in the *Menorah Journal* remarked, with somewhat more vigor than accuracy, that in Washington Square College, "where over ninety percent of the students are Jews, less than one percent of the instructors are Jewish." The same writer said, "Pressure on department heads from the old guard of the university has much to do with this fact. . . . Most of the Jewish teachers—there are about eight of them in the entire College—are only assistant instructors and will probably never go farther."

The complaint that there are only a few Jewish instructors in a Jewish-dominated college could be repeated literally and exactly concerning several of the night law schools.

The lower grade faculty positions in most of the big colleges are fairly open to Jews. The rub comes as they aspire toward advancement. A representation which begins promisingly on the ground floor seems to fade almost entirely before mounting to the peak of a professorship. Some Jews do advance by following the advice, "Go west, young man, go west."

There never has been a Jewish president of one of the better known American colleges, although the University of Missouri had a Jewish dean as acting president.

The group of subjects called the Humanities is particularly difficult for the Jewish teacher to enter. Ludwig Lewisohn in *Up Stream* discusses the matter plaintively, and he is not fictionizing. Jacob Zeitlin at the University of Illinois is one of a very few Jewish professors of English in the United States. There are no Jews in the English department at Princeton, none above the rank of instructor at Pennsylvania, although both Universities have a fair sprinkling in other subjects. Sociology, chemistry, and engineering are distinctively non-Jewish sciences. Anthropology—thanks to the influence of Professor Franz Boas of Columbia—economics, physics, and mathematics afford greater opportunities.

* * *

One of America's best advertised advocates of civil service reform in talking to a lieutenant cautioned him: "We must not extend the law too far—else we shall have nothing but Jews in the public employment." His analysis was keen. Jews have a particular aptitude for the examinations, much as the Scotch fill civil service positions in England.

So it happens that a high proportion of Jewish teachers are employed in New York City public schools, and a larger proportion of the grade school principals are Jews. They work their way upward by energy and aptitude through the ranks of the thirty thousand civil service employes of the school system. Their fate is in the hands of the Board of Examiners for Teachers, of which two members out of seven are Jewish, and the board has established a high reputation for fairness.

At the top is a little group of appointive officials in the most prized positions, and among them Jews are few. The first Jew ever appointed principal of a senior high school was Elias Lieberman, in 1924, and now there are four out of the forty senior high school principals. There are two Jewish district superintendents out of about forty. One Jew is among the nine members of the powerful Board of Associate Superintendents.

Whenever a complaint of prejudice is made against the Board of Examiners, it usually concerns the giving of the "n.g. list". That does not mean the "no good" list. It is a reading exercise for the weeding out of bad diction. New York, none too soon, has become self-conscious over its speech. It doesn't want its teachers saying "erl" for "oil", nor pronouncing words such as "singing" so that the "g" fizzes off in the middle of the next syllable as if exploded by a delayed time fuse. That tricky combination of "n" and "g" as in "finger" and "bringing", simple as it may seem, is a puzzle to the foreign-born tongue and ear. Many teachers have been eliminated thereby. But one could hardly call it discrimination.

Minor discriminations against Jews doubtless occur every year in the matter of assignment of teachers. School principals have a certain veto power as to whether they want the teachers sent them. There have been cases where the principal sought to exclude Jewish teachers. Sometimes the motive is unmasked and the principal is reprimanded; and at other times the undesirable teacher is sent elsewhere to another less, or more, desirable school.

Teaching in elementary schools outside the city is quite as difficult and precarious a vocation for Jews as college teaching. Rural communities, with a negligible Jewish population, desire teachers who will be conventional types. They desire characteristic suburbanites or Main Streeters, and the Jew is essentially urban. Outside school hours the men should be either athletic coaches or Boy Scout leaders, the women should be clubby, and on Sunday they all should go willingly to one of the leading Protestant churches as good examples to their pupils. Jewish teachers obviously do not fit the picture.

Accordingly, in the graduate school of education

at New York University, one finds a class of thirty working for higher degrees, with not a single Jew. Why should there be?

The experience of a Jew in teaching is illustrated in the story told by a professor at the College of the City of New York. One of his graduates after attaining fair success as manager of a store for a chain organization, decided to fit himself to be a teacher of mechanical drawing. He had mechanical aptitude and was interested in designing machines and improving parts.

"There was no opening for his type of work in the city system," recalled the professor. "He filled out applications at the various teachers' agencies, and answers came quickly and in gratifying number. From each letter he gathered that the job was his if conditions of salary were satisfactory.

"The letters which I saw pointed out the advantages offered by a particular community, urged the young man to come to teach, and then asked that as a matter of form, he fill out the enclosed blank. Invariably all negotiations ceased abruptly, for each of the blanks contained a question which asks very specifically, "What is your denominational affiliation?" Some contain two or three questions. One question asks "Have you ever changed your name?" or "What is your father's last name?" Others ask for birthplace of both parents and the like.

"This young man decided to talk the thing over

with the owner of one of the agencies. The owner explained that he was eager to be helpful, and then asked if he had ever heard of people who adopt children and thus become foster parents, or of people who adopt a new country. The young man replied that he had. 'Well,' said the owner of the agency, 'Why not adopt a new religion. Without this formality, I am afraid we cannot place you.' "

Continuing further, an inquiry concerning discrimination against Jews was made at one of the largest teachers' agencies in New York, specializing in out of town placements. "I have been at this business twenty-five years," said the manager. "I place hundreds of teachers every year. In all that time I have succeeded in landing positions for only six Jews."

Chapter VI

"GIVE A JOB TILL JUNE"

IN the spring of 1930 I undertook to set up what amounted to a free employment agency. My original notion had not included any such elaborate scheme. Having noticed, as everybody in New York did, the extraordinary number of people hanging around Sixth Avenue employment agencies, I felt something had to be done. Of course, there were at that time numerous agencies of one sort or another which undertook to bring the jobless and the job together. But it was a time at which very little publicity was being given to conditions of unemployment. In fact, official Washington had somewhat set a pattern, and this pattern included a minimization of existing difficulties. The theory was that if very little was said about unemployment, public confidence would be the more quickly restored. A number of political and industrial leaders sincerely believed that our difficulties were psychological. They felt that if it were possible to change the psychology, economic change would follow. But I felt that the trouble went deeper than a state of mind. Moreover, I couldn't help being stirred by the hardships of those who were physically cold and physically hungry even if the depression did happen to be psychological.

Of course, I had no notion that anything I might do would be more than a drop in the bucket. But I wanted to stir up my own community.

In the beginning, it began with a simple newspaper column in which I said that if anybody who needed a job would write in, and if anybody who had a job to give would also communicate with me, it might be possible to match up the need and the requirement. I had underestimated the extent of joblessness in New York. Within a few days five or six thousand letters had come in from people seeking work. Not more than twenty offers of jobs were received. Accordingly, it became necessary to organize a group of executive-minded and efficient people. Such a group was quickly obtained. I undertook to be the press agent of the organization and ballyhoo the movement by frequent radio talks over WMCA, and speeches at various clubs, churches, and synagogues. Naturally, with an organization, we had to have a slogan. And the alliterative title of "Give a Job till June" was chosen.

It was my notion that a certain amount of artificial work could be created in devising temporary jobs. Of course, I realized that if a real position were open it made little difference whether the applicant found his way to it through our organization or some other. Actual jobs generally find some available person. Our only utility as an employment agency lay in the creation of such jobs as were not wholly necessary. But above that, I did believe that our chief and most important function would be to call popular attention to the fact of unemployment.

We managed to place approximately a thousand people, but some of these jobs represented no more than a single day's work. And looking back on it, I am convinced that anything we could and did do, along these lines, was comparatively futile.

However, I did have an opportunity to learn a little about joblessness, particularly among the white collar workers. This is a phase of unemployment which is still neglected by economists and publicists. You don't hear much about it. The white collar worker is not organized to any effective extent, and he is not articulate. He may, in course of time, come to the breadline or the Municipal lodging house, but this is rare. As a rule he—and I had better add she by now—goes on living. Frequently the jobless white collar worker is dependent on the good will of family or friends. There is the process of going in to live with somebody else. In a sense it is the most desperate and dangerous kind of unemployment, because a laborer out of a job, if he is single, goes down alone. The white collar worker pulls another with him. His dependence upon friend or family may depress an entire group somewhat below the level of reasonably decent living conditions.

And, of course, it was among the white collar workers that we found the severest sort of religious discrimination. Generally speaking, the skilled mechanic or the laborer is not much handicapped by being Jewish. You can dig a ditch without ever having the problem of your religion come up. You can usually run a machine and not face this question—that is, unless it is a typewriting machine. Once an applicant enters an office where he is to keep books, take dictation, or manifold manuscripts or circulars, his boss wants to know something about his church. Even the mere matter of putting stamps on an envelope is not considered a wholly secular occupation in New York.

* * *

I began my career as head of an employment agency by saying: "In this office, at least, we will ask no man or woman about his race or religious affiliations. And we will allow no employer to ask." It was much easier said than done. In fact, even my own passionate belief in complete equality was dented somewhat by existing conditions which I had to face. I remember one large firm said it would take two stenographers from us. I told our office manager to supply this need. And I said, "This is a big organization and if we send them satisfactory people, they may take more. Pick out the best you have." He sent two girls for the job and neither of them was accepted. I was disappointed, and the next day we sent two others, who also were turned away disconsolate. At this point our office manager said to me, "You will just have to face the facts, Mr. Broun. This organization you're dealing with has an unwritten rule that it won't employ Jews. And you say I am not to ask anybody on our list about his religion. What do you want to do now?"

My first impulse was to say, "Well, let's have no dealings with that firm." But yet, I knew that we had among our applicants Gentile stenographers to whom we had promised that we would do our very best to find a position. And here were jobs which we might fill. Accordingly, under pressure, I did compromise without breaking the rule about asking any applicant her religious faith. I told the office manager to pick out for this particular job, girls who had non-Jewish names and were non-Jewish in appearance. Two satisfactory applicants were finally sent. Of course, I don't know that they actually were Gentile. They merely looked that way. Quite a few corporations which have a prejudice against Jewish employes decide on somewhat the same basis, without actually asking a religious test question.

Having confessed this much about my own employment agency I must go on to acquit the commercial agencies of being necessarily biased. They, too, have to meet conditions as they find them. I had one letter from a stenographer who had been to fifteen agencies, and not one would even take the trouble to list her as an applicant. Finally, at one agency she was told frankly, "I'm sorry, but I might as well tell you that at the present time we are getting no call for Jewish workers. If we sent you around to any of the jobs which are open, we would simply be wasting your time as well as our own."

* * *

Of course, I can't prove it by precise statistics, but it is my impression that the number of companies going in for "Christians Only" increased very radically during the period of depression when there was a large over-supply of office workers. During this time I wrote a piece in the *Evening Telegram* in which I said that I would give a bright, new dime to anybody who would send me a convincing letter in justification of discrimination against Jews in office work. I received a number of letters, and none was convincing, although many were long and detailed. A very familiar explanation was that the Jewish employe was inclined to discuss the secrets of the firm with outsiders, and that in many instances he might go to a rival company carrying with him confidential knowledge such as names of customers, mailing lists, and so on. But I never received any specific testimony to this effect. It was always in highly generalized terms. It was also the complaint that the Jewish worker was restless, overly ambitious, and constantly trying to undermine the man who stood immediately over him in the office scale. Then there was that very old one about uncouthness and vulgarity, and one or two writers who said that they were employers maintaining their own freedom from prejudice, but added that there was much bickering in the office force if some workers were Jewish and some Gentile.

I discussed the general trend of these letters with Rabbi Wise, who told me that he thought only one charge had any substantiality. "I admit," he said, "that the Jewish worker is restless and ambitious. He wants to go ahead and to be doing something else." He said that whenever you read an obituary notice of a man who had worked with one concern for forty-five years as a bookkeeper, the chances would be that this particular worker was a Gentile. I supplemented the rabbi's statement by adding that I thought this was true. After all, it is the Christian church which has urged the individual to be satisfied with that state of life to which it has pleased God to call him, and in the minds of many Gentiles there may arise a certain confusion between God and the Universal Pump Company. If a man stays without complaint, without question, without plea for preferment, in the same cubbyhole for forty years, finally to be buried in East Orange under a cross of white lilies sent by the firm, depend upon it he is not Jewish.

Yet, I can hardly see that a dog-like devotion

should be considered a mark of high ability in an office worker. After all, no business man ever makes a speech at a banquet or to the immediate members of his office family, without saying that the firm welcomes advice and cooperation, that it expects every young man and woman in the place to improve himself, and to get ahead. If the Jewish worker takes these exhortations at their face value, and is restless (which, after all, is merely a synonym for ambitious), and does try to learn things outside his immediate niche so that he may obtain promotion, why should he be blamed? Surely, nobody has a right to say that this is an alien and a foreign state of mind. American industry has been vitalized for fifty years on the various stories of success—it is the success of the young man who started at the bottom and worked his way to the top of the ladder. We take pride in mentioning the fact that Henry Ford tinkered with bicycles; that Chrysler was in a harness shop; that Schwab rose from the ranks.

So deeply has this theory of the emergence of the underling been hammered down, that even on the breadline or in the municipal lodging house you will find men completely satisfied with the economic status of America, because they feel secure in the belief that all they need is a break. Some day—and that not too distant—their feet will be set in the pathway which leads up and up to Park Avenue pent houses. It is true, probably, that the Jewish citizen more than any other has, on occasion, made these fabulous tales come true in part. The field of real estate is filled with instances of the immigrant or the immigrant's son who has come up from push-cart days to finance and control the erection of great skyscrapers. In fact, the sky line of New York has been traced by the fingers of men who still contain within their palms the callouses of days on the lowest rung. It is curious that a nation which takes such pride in the Ford or the Schwab story cannot be excited by the tale of a Benjamin Winter.

The barrier against the Jewish worker extends to department store helpers. A saleswoman may be gravely handicapped if she is obviously Jewish, and even in some of the department stores which are controlled by Jewish business men there is discrimination. Here, another factor enters in which is not founded directly on either race or religion. For some reason wholly unknown to me, department store proprietors want their young women to be blonde—and natural blondes are preferred. Walk through the aisles of any big New York store, and you will find at least ten blondes to every brunette. I doubt if nature goes this far. A great majority of Jewish young women are not blonde. Here comes still an additional handicap. One department store is said to have a curious rule that on the ground floor all the employes shall be Gentile. Race prejudice ends as the elevator goes up.

* * *

Here, for instance, is a typical letter which came in response to my columnar requests for letters explaining any sound reasons for race prejudice:

> "Dear Mr. Broun:
>
> I won't lay claim to that new dime you offer because I cannot give a good reason for religious discrimination in business. I can, however, give you some of the reasons of those who do discriminate. The most prevalent explanations that I have found amongst business men of their dislike of Jews is that they consider Jews to be uncouth, unmannerly, unscrupulous individuals. Some business men have complained that Jewish employes are too quick to take an unfair advantage, that they have no hesitancy to lie or cheat. I have heard them go so far as to accuse them of downright dishonesty and say that a Jew cannot be trusted. I have also heard the complaint made that when a Jew gets into a firm he tries to bring in all of his relatives and friends, more particularly his relatives, and, as it were, pack the place with his own kind.
>
> However, whatever their reasons, the

> same firms that refuse to hire Jews will not only sell goods to Jewish customers but do it on extremely liberal credit terms.
>
> One of the sad phases of this religious discrimination is that daily in New York City thousands of Jewish job seekers commit perjury in order to get jobs. Knowing in advance that a Jewish name or an admission that they are Jews will bar them from employment, they change their names and masquerade as members of other religions, running all the way from Catholic to Christian Scientist. Many of those who succeed by such a subterfuge work under the constant fear that they will be found out and consequently discharged.
>
> What employers do not seem to realize is that by setting up an arbitrary religious barrier they are depriving themselves of a high type of ability and business initiative, and hence suffer a loss that can be computed in dollars and cents."

I don't know whether this particular writer is Jewish or Gentile, but he falls into what seems to me a curious error in regard to the change of name which he refers to as perjury. This is certainly wholly unjustified since the law admits the right of every individual to take whatever name happens to please him, the only limitations being that he may not call himself Tiffany and set up a jewelry store under that name, or seek to avoid existing obligations. The notion that a name is legally unchangeable except through court action, probably rests upon the practice of appealing to a judge for permission to change. But this is a legal fiction. One need not ask any such sanction. Indeed, one of the best known judges in America told me that courts had no rights in such matters which the citizen need respect. He said, "If a man comes to me and asks permission to change his name, I may refuse for some whimsical cause or other, but that doesn't bar him from going straight from my court and changing it any way. I can do nothing about it."

Nor is the practice of changing the name confined to Jewish residents in New York. I might cite the fact that many Germans whose names sound awkward avail themselves of the process of adopting a more euphonious cognomen. And in some cases you run into the fact of a foreign name that may either approximate American slang or coincide with an obscene word in our language, in which case only the most captious person would object to a change. The stage is crowded with young men and women who have decided that they came to the business with labels too cumbersome or too unromantic and have seized upon more fetching titles for themselves. Professional baseball has shown many examples of the same process. Within recent years a number of Polish players have come to the big league. In some cases shortening of the name was not even their own decision. The necessity of newspaper space and the limitation of the box score may easily reduce a Peckinpaugh to Peck whether he chooses it or not. And when he has become through newspaper circulation Peck to millions of baseball fans, Peck he will remain and not Peckinpaugh.

* * *

Hundreds of letters written to me by jobless people during that employment agency experience testified vividly to the prejudice against Jews. Here is one which is fairly typical of what was reported and how it impressed the one discriminated against:

> "I was very much interested in your short talk last night on the unemployment situation, simply because I have been out of work for three weeks and the outlook isn't very promising. . . . It seems that the only outstanding reason I am unable to connect, is the fact that I am a Jew. If you expect to give us another one of your talks in the near future, it wouldn't be a bad idea to emphasize the fact that Jews are also human and must eat.
>
> "I am twenty-three, have had six years experience in secretarial and stenographical

detail—all of which I find, means nothing, having been born a Jew.

"Having made my rounds of the employment agencies for the time already mentioned, I find that there are positions to be had—provided your religion is satisfactory.

"Yesterday I went into an agency on 5th Avenue for the first time. The reception I received was something like this 'We *never* have an opening for Jewish girls, so it would be useless for you to register.' This morning I received a letter from a soap company. I had answered one of their ads. The lady who interviewed me seemed to be very well pleased with my knowledge of office routine. However, the gentleman for whom I was to work was a little 'peculiar' to quote her own words, and preferred to work with someone of his own religion.

"Every Jewish girl who is out of work in New York City today is being humiliated in this manner daily, and there doesn't seem to be quite a good reason for it. Can you offer any?

"I can truthfully boast of just as much refinement and good breeding as some of my Christian colleagues, and strange to relate, I get just as hungry as they do."

Here's a quotation from another letter:

"But, being Jewish, I'm having a hell of a time getting a job. Where do you Gentiles get that stuff calling us 'God's Chosen People'? We're certainly not being chosen for jobs here in New York. We realize the sense of the motheaten bromide of 'Many are called, but few are chosen.' In other words, I've (and, aren't we (Jews) all?) been called for interviews, but not been chosen."

And still another:

"I find that the fact that I am a Jew is held against me although why I cannot say. I come from a good family who were all born here. Three generations ago, my family came from Germany. My parents and three of my grandparents were born in this country. Yet when I say I am American many employers eye me askance."

Chapter VII

JEWS AND JOBS

Two apparently conflicting items seem at first to confuse the question of the existence and extent of discrimination against Jews in employment in New York.

Exhibit A consists of the want ad sections of the newspapers. For practical study, they should have been examined before the unemployment slump of the spring of 1930 when the "Help Wanted" columns dwindled away to small resemblance to their former size. An innocent visitor from the country glancing over these advertisements would have been delighted by their testimony to the piety of employers, and the interest they took in the spiritual welfare of their help.

In the *Times* on one single Sunday, a rapid count showed sixty-nine advertisements which considered religion a sufficiently vital quality in the life of an employe to make special inquiry about it. Most of these used some such phraseology as "state age, education, experience, salary expected, and religion." The *World* on the same day also asked about religion, but went farther on occasion and requested

"Christians". It did not specify between fundamentalists and modernists, high church or low church, immersionists, Calvinists, or holy rollers—leaving such matters to the individual conscience. There were thirty-four of these inquiries in the *World*. The *Herald-Tribune* made twenty such inquiries, many of them specifying "Protestants", while the *American* carried two, one asking for a "Christian", the other requesting applicants to "state religion". One of the papers in an ad for a grocery boy specified—"must ride bicycle. Jewish boy preferred."

"Well, well," might be the thought of our visitor from the country. "They have been telling me of the Godless city, yet more than a hundred employers in one day come out publicly, and buy advertising space to signify their faith in religion. New York seems after all to be in a state of grace. Here is something to tell the folks back home."

So religion is the word, the formula. It might be called race or nationality. At any rate, the meaning applies to Jews. Employers are telling Jewish workers that it isn't worth while to apply for jobs. They are announcing what amounts to an economic boycott.

Employers are not interested in the religion of their people, of course; care not whether they worship the Holy Trinity, Jehovah, Allah or Mammon. Discrimination enters the mind in New York not because the object goes to the synagogue or temple, and not definitely in resentment because he is of the seed of Abraham. Jewish individuals here represent every degree of orthodoxy. They are gathered from Spain and Germany and Russia; from Palestine and Hungary and England. They bring a blood mixed with many other strains of mankind, and customs picked up in all the nations of the world. The word Jew is merely a sort of identification today, just as was the yellow badge prescribed in the Middle Ages. Jews may be defined as accurately as any other way, perhaps, by calling them the heirs of a certain tradition. Calling the commonly observed prejudice religious or racial is but a convenient definition for feeling against a more or less exotic minority, which serves as an outlet for community blame and irritation. It simply tags these diverse people for our broad generalization, "They are all Jews, and we don't want Jews."

Exhibit B, on the other hand, is a famous cartoon from the *New Yorker* magazine. It shows a canyon of tall buildings in New York with not one person visible on the street. Its title is "Yom Kippur". It certainly is near enough to the truth to be funny. The traffic problem is relieved noticeably on days when Jews don't go to work.

Well then, if that is so, what becomes of this alleged economic boycott? One answer is that the cartoon is much more accurate for the clothing district, around Seventh Avenue and Thirty-sixth

Street, than for many other sections. But not all the Jews are garment workers. It has been estimated, indeed, that every seventeenth person you pass on the street in Manhattan is a garment worker, and thinning out the crowd by so much would do wonders for many a street corner. There's a saying, too, that every garment man goes eventually into real estate—or into Wall Street, or the theatre business. But in every part of the city and in every activity one finds busy and well-fed Jews. They personally weren't boycotted, were they? Thousands of them, naturally, operate their own independent businesses, large or small, or work for other Jews. (However, some employment agencies estimate that as high as fifty percent of the Jewish-owned offices and business houses restrict, or entirely refuse, employes of their own race.) Thousands of others have found entry into Gentile concerns.

The tallest hurdle in the path of a Jew is the initial getting of a job. Once at work, he may feel that race and religion still are a crushing handicap, and advancement undoubtedly is more difficult for him. But he can take comfort that it is easier to keep a job than to get it. Even here, though, he is under a disadvantage. In good times when there are many jobs, even a Jew may find employment. When times are hard, Jews often are the first to be laid off, and then the last to be taken on again. Jews are more susceptible than other classes to the ups and downs of the labor market. The rapid turnover of Jewish employes, often cited against them, is not entirely of their own making.

To answer this question: "Are Jews really boycotted, and is there discrimination against them in employment?" is the purpose of this chapter. That, and also to sketch something of the causes and extent of the boycott. The answer, in advance, is "Yes". The labor market may fluctuate, but it is true as a compass to one guiding principle. It never drops its exaggerated sales resistance to the Jewish applicant.

* * *

The want ad sections of the papers are probably the frankest acknowledgment of the sharp discrimination in employment. And exclusion from jobs is the most widespread of all anti-Jewish manifestations. It causes more actual hardship and bitterness than any of the other forms of prejudice.

New York is not alone in this practice. A recent study in Philadelphia quoted help wanted columns as saying:

"SALESMAN—With good appearance and reference, to solicit savings accounts for bank. A good opportunity. Gentile, under forty-five preferred."

Also:

"YOUNG LADIES—Eighteen to twenty-three, Gentile, for advertising work; must travel in auto with group of girls; salary and expense arrangement."

This discrimination is widespread and in nowise lessening. The New York papers no longer use insulting language. There was a time when hotels advertised "No Jews or Dogs Permitted", and when the want ad said "No Jews need apply", "Christians only", and even more pointed phrases.

Then came a reform in manners. For a time no discriminatory words at all were permitted by the newspapers. Then it was discovered that this was no service to the Jew himself. With no indication in the advertisement whether prejudice existed or not, the poor Jew was kept chasing all over the city, running his legs off, in pursuit of job prospects which proved hopeless for one of his race. Many employers who discriminate against Jews in fact still do not announce it through the papers, so there is enough wasted effort at best. Gradually the damning but enlightening phrases crept back. The *Times* censorship does not permit advertising for "Christians", but it approves "Christian firm desires stenographer." There is nothing against asking the applicant to "state race", or "nationality", or "nationality of both parents". Other catch phrases used in the papers include "Only refined Americans need apply", "social references required", occasionally

"Gentile". All these translate into the very definite rule of Christians only, Jews keep out. They are designed to prevent waste of time upon useless material, to save the personal embarrassment of saying face to face to the applicant, "Our quota is filled," or else bluntly, "We don't employ Jews; it's a rule of the firm."

Out of twenty-four items in half a column of "Help Wanted—Female" ads in the *World,* twelve or exactly half indicated racial exclusion. One employment agency dealing in office help began its ad with the line "Christians! Christians!" while another carried in large type, over a list of available positions, "American Christians only."

A Jewish stenographer or clerk setting out to hunt work and reading the want ads, therefore, receives promptly a lesson in the disadvantage of being a Jew. Here is the first suggestion to change the name, to abandon the religion, to give up the birthright and attempt the difficult evasion of "passing". Hence is born a new generation of outlaws from their race.

* * *

A second lesson in discrimination comes as the job-seeker visits the employment agencies. Some refuse to register Jews, tactless representatives not uncommonly tearing up the card before the eyes of the applicant upon discovery that he is Jewish. Other agencies discourage Jewish applicants, while even the most friendly are inclined to point out that placement is going to be a little more difficult than for a Gentile. The agencies themselves are not so much influenced by personal prejudice as by the employers with whom they deal. They find it unprofitable to interview and register hundreds for whom there is slight probability of getting jobs. The agency sees no commission in applicants it cannot place; it sees no prestige in the eyes of employers from sending applicants who will not be acceptable. It knows that this employer says frankly, "Don't send me any Jews," that another has a quota.

This shifting of responsibility from agency to employer goes a step further. The employer shifts it on to the public, making the situation almost a circle and certainly vicious. Many employers who refuse Jews disclaim personal antipathy. They say, "It's none of my business what a worker's race or religion may be. I have no feeling. But so many customers or clients don't like Jews. We can't keep satisfactory relations outside if we have Jews to make the contact. We'd take Jews, but our public won't stand for them."

An agency recently displayed the sign in its office, "No Jewish Applications Until Further Notice." This was ordered removed by the city department of licenses. Another posted the typewritten statement:

NOTICE TO NEW JEWISH APPLICANTS

We accept applications only from twenty dollars to twenty-five dollars a week Jewish stenographers (the twenty dollar stenographers must have had at least two years experience) and from RAPID Jewish typists.

We CANNOT accept applications from Jewish bookkeepers, assistant bookkeepers, medium or slow speed typists, clerks and other classes of office workers, as we get no calls for them.

Those leaving an application with us MUST wait upon a phone call or letter before calling again. We are glad to notify them when we get suitable calls, but must restrict their visits in order to keep down our traffic.

NOTE: The Associated Placement Bureau, 1451 Broadway (corner 41st Street) have asked us to call your attention to the fact that they specialize in the placing of Jewish applicants.

* * *

Employment agencies unconsciously recognize the handicap of Jewishness by their private designations. Most agency blanks for recording jobs available have place for a "Code Number". In this space, 1 means Protestant, 2 means Catholic, 3 means Jew. A zero means the employer did not specify. This code is not universally followed, but it is safe to say none of the agencies call a Jew an A 1 prospect.

Some of them call Jews "fives". This term came from a more elaborate system of grading. An average employe was known as a "three"; better than average, "two"; an altogether exceptional prospect, "one". On the other hand, a sub-average applicant was a "four" and one scarcely desirable at all, "five". From this developed the designation by race and religion which calls just the average nondescript "three", a Protestant "one", a Catholic "two", an Italian or other foreigner "four", and a Jew "five".

It is a good system. It enables agencies and employers in the know to discuss applicants frankly and without embarrassment in their very presence. Furthermore, it is extremely logical.

A code system is used, apparently, by large employers also. Some of them rather pride themselves upon not asking the race or religion upon their questionnaires for prospective employes. Yet they often have a covert religious classification. The Consolidated Gas Company has no such question upon its blank. However, in the upper left-hand corner there is a small block of four squares lined off, numbered 1, 2, 3, 4. As the applicant is given the blank by a personnel agent, he is asked orally what his religion is, and a notation is made on the reserved space. The record there is only a series of tiny check marks, plus or minus signs, and letters.

Employment agency managers agree that discrimination against Jews reaches its peak in New York City. Gertrude R. Stein, who operates her own Vocational Service Agency, reported that in Boston there was no marked discrimination against Jews, but there was against Catholics somewhat comparable to that against Jews in New York. Jews from other cities, particularly from the South, coming to work in New York are baffled and crushed at first by the rebuffs which they receive.

The attitude of the agencies is discussed in a report of the Bureau of Jewish Social Research on the survey which it completed in June, 1929. Discussing the twenty-three commercial agencies studied, the summary says:

> "One flatly refused to register any Jews; another stated that he could place no Jews; eight more were very discouraging and emphasized the futility of registering since Jewish girls stood no chance of being placed.
>
> "Seven were willing to register the girls but explained that there would be difficulty in placing them since so many employers

did not want Jews; six of the agencies were encouraging and asked the girls to register, assuring them that some jobs would be found in the near future and that there was little discrimination against them. In brief, in ten out of twenty-three agencies the Jewish girls had no chance of being placed; at seven they had very little chance and at only six they had as good a chance as if they were not Jewish.

"According to some of the employment agencies such discrimination is found among Jewish professional and business people as well as among non-Jewish, and the agencies must meet the demands of the employers."

* * *

Refusals to give an applicant a chance just because he or she is a Jew run into the tens of thousands. There are doubtless hundreds of thousands of other refusals from which the applicant goes away thinking he has encountered prejudice but which have a different basis. As Jewish social research students, themselves, point out, discrimination does constitute the first and most convenient excuse with which a Jew may salve his wounds after failing to get what he wants. Being refused a job, the applicant says at once, "It was because I am a

Jew," and thereby avoids the suggestion that he is in any sense less qualified than the chosen person. This self-deception and natural tendency to shift the blame make it difficult to place a finger upon any one experience as being one hundred percent prejudice. Yet there are many which seem to exhibit no other motive. Here is such a case, reported in a letter dated April 6, 1930:

> "Last Friday I was interviewed by the president of a large laundry concern in Brooklyn. After a half hour talk he employed me, asking me to report for work the following Monday. As I was leaving he said, 'Oh, by the way, you're not Jewish? I ask because so many Jewish girls come in here.'
>
> "He was very much taken aback when I told him, 'I am.' He seemed angry at himself not to have asked the question before, but told me nevertheless to come in Monday. But the following day—Saturday—a special messenger brought the enclosed letter."

The laundryman's letter said:

> "This is to notify you that you need not report for work Monday morning as I

> have made other arrangements which I think will answer my requirements better."

Another letter from a stenographer, dated February 4, 1930, tells of having been employed in the general offices of a large Jewish-owned real estate firm which also builds and operates hotels. Before one of their swanky new places just off Park Avenue was opened, she was assigned as secretary to the manager there. But after it opened, she was sent back to the general offices. The manager professed to be anxious to retain her. Her disappointment was given the cold comfort of an explanation that the firm employed Jews only behind the scenes, never out in their hotels where they would meet the public.

A letter on the stationery of the executive offices of a nationally-known corporation was kindly forwarded by the recipient. It was sent out by special delivery, and said:

> "Dear Sir:
>
> If not already engaged, kindly call in person, Tuesday, July 22nd, between the hours of 9 and 12 A.M., in connection with your advertisement appearing in the *New York Times,* Sunday, July 20, 1930.
>
> Christians only need apply.
>
> Yours very truly,
>
> MERGENTHALER LINOTYPE COMPANY."

Such personal experiences quite naturally persuade thousands of Jews to deny their race and religion and change their names. Sometimes they are able by that means to obtain jobs otherwise barred to them.

A personal friend described her own experience as a Jewish girl first beginning to look for work in New York. She and another girl had been all around, everywhere being asked "What is your religion," and being turned down—they thought because they were Jews. They decided never again to make the fatal admission. The next place the employment agency sent them, they met the same old question and answered, "We believe in the brotherhood of man." Refusal again.

"You little fools," said the man at the agency when they returned. "That place specified that they wanted Jewish girls."

Nearly every Jewish congregation in the city has members who insist and demand that no bulletin or other literature be sent to their business address to connect them in any way with a synagogue.

The rabbi of a prominent congregation was interrupted in his study by the old man who was washing his windows. Pious and orthodox, the window washer wanted to tell his distress over his two sons. He wept for them. They had gone and joined a Lutheran church.

They did not actually believe as the Lutherans

did. They had not in their hearts repudiated their own faith, he consoled himself. But they were almost as bad.

"But how could they get jobs, if they didn't?" he asked. When it was discovered that they were Jews, they were refused. If they said they were Christians and were not, the bosses checked up and discharged them. So the boys took no more chances. They applied for membership in the Lutheran church and were accepted. Now if any employer asks their religion, they glibly reel off the name and telephone number of the Lutheran pastor. If this be called a "Jew trick", how can the Gentile escape responsibility for it?

The Lutheran church, according to employment agencies, is the one named most often in answering the religion query by Jews who think to evade the discrimination. However, they answer all the well-known names as to their church, not only Methodist, Baptist, Presbyterian, Catholic, but also Atheist, Protestant, Gentile.

Some of the answers reveal a pathetic, striving ignorance. One agency has the application card of an eighteen-year-old Jewish girl seeking a job as stenographer and asking fifteen dollars a week, who filled out the questions: nationality - American; religion - French.

Some of the agencies friendly to Jews frankly advised those whose features and appearance are not of strongly Jewish type to deny their race and take a new name. They promise employment much sooner and with far less difficulty if they will change over from Greenberg to Gordon.

In this connection, a want ad of blunt honesty is the subject of comment by Charles H. Joseph in the *American Israelite* (Cincinnati) of April 25, 1930. He writes:

> "Well, some of us have imagination, and a little daring. Here's an ad that was handed to me from *Printer's Ink* that is so unusual that it's worth reprinting. Then, too, it tells the old story of prejudice that is far too common in the business world. The text of the ad is:

> A JEW
>
> Can any one use this executive as an Advertising or Sales Promotion Manager? A man who will bring you unimpeachable loyalty, integrity and proven ability. A man who through the traits of his heritage can give you value, service and dependability that cannot be purchased. Such a man will be available soon, as prejudicial working conditions demand a change.
>
> 'Address "E", Box 227, Printer's Ink.'

"Nothing like nailing one's flag to the mast," continued Mr. Joseph. "Sometimes I think that the parents of Yehudi Menuhin were right when they decided to name him 'Yehudi' so that no one would ever take him for other than a Jew!"

* * *

Discrimination against Jews in New York spreads all over the city, reaches like a dark cloud into the narrowest and most remote streets, to the largest and smallest lines of employment. It is practiced deliberately, and also unconsciously, by those who dislike Jews and by those who don't care but who yield to a supposed demand by the public. It is of vast proportions and it is by no means decreasing.

Here is the testimony of figures as found at the alumni employment service maintained by a great university. It reported that three months after graduation, the members of a recent class still without jobs were referred as a routine procedure to the bureau. It was noted that although Jews constituted only fifteen percent of the total class membership, approximately forty percent of those still unplaced were Jews.

The percentage against Jews in employment is brought out again in the experience of the Vocational Service for Juniors, a free, non-sectarian placement organization located in the East Side of New York under the direction of Dr. Mary H. S. Hayes. The Service recently took a look backward over ten years of work during which it had received applications from 27,000 youngsters, of whom 38 percent were Jews, 50 percent Catholics, 10 percent Protestants and two percent indicating no religion.

Jobs were found for 44 percent of all applicants —nearly 12,000 jobs. But jobs were found for only 20 percent of the Jewish applicants. That is, it was considerably more than twice as difficult to find a job for a Jewish applicant as for the average.

The point is strengthened by this additional fact: the Jewish applicants were educationally better qualified for the jobs. The figures showed that 37 percent of all the Jewish applicants between 14 and 18 years old had had some high school training, while only 18 percent of the Gentiles had been to high school.

The service recognized one important factor in addition to race in this apparent discrimination against Jews. Jewish girls as a class do not want factory jobs; they want to work in offices. With the strong will of the downtrodden for advancement, they desire the more dignified white-collar jobs. Of all Jewish girls enrolled, 70 percent refused any except office work. This fact makes a considerable cut in the figures for discrimination, but it is a long way from a complete explanation of it. An examination of 2,289 calls at the service revealed 614 or 26.8 percent who specified non-Jews.

Although many Jewish employment specialists favor the increased establishment of Jewish agencies to concentrate on the problem, Dr. Hayes disagrees. No employer who thinks he does not want Jewish help will pay any attention to a Jewish agency, according to her reasoning. An agency having applicants of all races, upon whose judgment the employer has come to rely, sometimes can persuade him to make a trial of some particularly suitable applicant, even though Jewish.

The strain of discrimination runs through all classifications of jobs, although, naturally, those which require the greatest training, and are most difficult to fill, place greater stress upon technical fitness and less upon personal qualities. In this they are recognizing nothing more than the scarcity of supply. Farther down the scale, competition is more bitter, and it is scant consolation to tell a Jew that he is welcome to any job which Gentiles do not consider desirable.

* * *

Now why all this discrimination? Why is he kicked out or the door slammed in his face? There must be some reason for it.

Easy, you say; Jews are terrible. People don't like them. Or, you say, Jews are a Freudian outlet. Or you offer a hundred other explanations or defamations. The word 'easy', at any rate, is the wrong word. It is a complex affair.

The reason for discrimination in employment most often given is the Jewish religious holidays. It is inconvenient to have the worker absent. And it is complained that on the holy days many absentees don't go to the synagogue but to the ball game.

The high holidays mean from two to five days a year on which other employes, non-Jewish, would work. A Jew of strict religious practice observing a full program of holidays would take the first and second days of the Rosh Hashanah celebration and one day for the near-by Yom Kippur in the fall, and the first and last days of the Passover season in the spring. A Jew of any pretense to religious conformity would take at least two holidays, the first day of Rosh Hashanah, and Yom Kippur. Intensely orthodox Jews do not work on Saturday. This classification, known as "Sabbath-observers", presents particular difficulties in employment, but rejection of them is not exactly prejudice. They find places, on the whole, with firms of Sabbath-observers, and all refrain from work together.

Of course, if half the telephone girls, the restaurant waitresses, the department store salespeople, walked off their jobs for even one day, it would throw an unequal burden upon the remainder. The employment agencies, however, in the role of impartial referees, usually rate the "holiday" objection to Jews as a subterfuge. Many workers offer to take no salary for their religious holidays off, a smaller number agree not to observe the holidays at all. Still they do not get jobs.

One fundamental reason for discrimination, as discussed with, and explained by, an experienced Gentile student of employment, lies in what is perhaps a racial characteristic of sticking up for one's own rights. Jews resist more than most people the little impositions which most employers practice for convenient operation. When the boss asks a Jew to stay an hour later to finish up some work, he refuses. He must go to night school. When advance agreements as to salary are not kept, Jews protest. They are not pliable help. Especially in the years past, they were known as organizers of labor unions. And so employers prefer more docile types, easier to manage. On the other hand, these very characteristics make them uncommonly valuable influences in the whole social structure of the working group, and Gentile workers get the benefit of agitations for which the Jewish worker is fired.

One of the most thorough studies of the causes of employment discrimination against Jews was made by Bruno Lasker, and published in the *Jewish Social Service Quarterly* of March, 1926. This was based upon direct questions to employers who advertised that they would not take Jews. Among the replies were the following:

> "Because all our employes are Christians."

Another:

> "Our past experience has proved that Jews and Gentiles do not work together very well, and the former we never found remarkable for cleanliness, etc."

Another:

> "One only needs to employ the other kind to find out. If you do not believe it, try it. Anyone sending out such a letter as this is not worthy of receiving a Christian's confidence."

A manufacturer of hospital supplies—himself foreign-born—said:

> "I hire Christian people because I myself am a Christian and will always give preference to members of my own race whenever it is in my power to do so. I feel that this is a duty of mine."

Commenting upon the answers, Mr. Lasker found

prejudice rather than reason at the heart of many. Said he:

> "In a majority of cases we are driven back again upon current social attitudes. . . . Of course efficiency in shop and office requires a certain amount of congeniality to make the work go smoothly; but the plea that race discrimination makes for congeniality has not, so far as we know, been put to a single scientific test. In fact, choice for congeniality in most cases is interpreted to mean broad distinctions along lines of popular assumptions as regards race characteristics; there is no personal examination of the applicant for a position to determine his eligibility from this point of view.
>
> "Thus firms that spend thousands of dollars upon testing supplies often apply no test at all to the hiring of a new worker, as regards his ability to get on with the rest, but choose by such irrelevant data as his name and the shape of his nose.
>
> "It is not surprising, therefore, if an employer who has been following a sentiment or half-realized prejudice in excluding Jews from his personnel is hard put to

> it when asked for an explanation and grabs at the first one that comes into his head, usually exaggerating some experience of his own or merely repeating some specific thing he has heard to the discredit of Jews."

Mr. Lasker summarizes his opinion by saying Jews are the victims of "a false generalization which then becomes repeated and handed on until in the popular Gentile view the whole Jewish race is charged with mental and moral qualities which, as a matter of plain, historical fact, are not characteristic of it at all."

The wide extent and persistence of business discrimination against Jews is blamed in part upon the employment agencies, by the Jewish manager of one which deals largely with Jewish applicants.

"I know how the agencies work from both ends of the telephone, for I was myself employment manager for a large concern for several years," he said. "I never called an agency to ask for help that I was not asked, 'Do you prefer Christians or do you mind if we send Jews?'

"This policy puts the question directly into the mind of the employer. It suggests that he discriminate. It may be only practical business for the agency, although it is not necessary in any case, but it works directly to the injury of the Jewish applicant.

" 'Do you object to Jews?' The question invites discrimination. On that very account, I believe many firms are listed as refusing Jews who otherwise would give them a fair chance on merit. My experience has proved this."

Another cause of discrimination pointed out by several agencies is this: it is a device to save time. As one agency manager said:

"Whenever an employer says he will take Jews, I say 'Heaven help him,' for he will be swamped by applicants. There are so many out of work, they need jobs so badly that the employer is almost liable to be trampled in the rush."

If there were no widespread ban against Jews, of course, this exaggerated tension would not exist. On the other hand, the employer who refuses to interview Jews insures himself a smaller number of applicants to bother with. He feels he can find a satisfactory person within the limited class. Another agency man reported, "Knowing the town as I do, when a stranger calls up and says, 'Send me just one applicant who will do for this job; I don't want to have to see any more,' why of course, I send a non-Jew."

The manager of one agency in discussing prejudice went so far in his definition as to say that an arbitrary refusal to employ any Jews so long as Gentiles were available would not amount to prejudice. The sight-unseen selection of Mr. Smith and rejection of Mr. Cohen would not be prejudice. There is no unfair prejudice, he held, until an employer absolutely refused to take a qualified Jewish person when he had exhausted every effort and failed to find a qualified Gentile. This argument, obviously, is but the measure of the prejudice in his own mind.

In looking at the employment problem, one realizes quickly that "qualifications" and proficiency for duties are the smallest element in fitting a person to a job. The problem is to "sell" the employer on the personality of the applicant. The employer feels sure he has the right to be satisfied with the kind of person who works for him. Who can deny him? If he wishes to set up an arbitrary rule that all the waitresses in his restaurant shall be redheaded, that all his cashiers shall be Scotch, that all his porters shall be a certain shade of mulatto, hasn't he the right? Wherein is this less wrongful than refusal to hire Jews?

If a Baptist deacon refuses to employ any but Baptists, it might be called an extreme case of prejudice. He is not picking types for any studied effect of atmosphere or color scheme that he wishes to produce; he simply is selecting his own kind of people with whom he thinks he can work most congenially. He is recognizing a factor which he considers highly important. Such cases of religious discrimination are rather common in the South and Middle West. In many a town there is a grocer, a pillar of the church, Methodist, Presbyterian, or Catholic, who just naturally employs all his sales clerks and delivery boys from his own communion. No others need apply.

Prejudice? Certainly. Has he a right to it? Certainly—there is no law to stop him. No one of his neighbors would say, however, that his policy is good for the community, which has everything to gain from the free flow of good feeling and human fellowship. Where, then, does one draw the line across which the legal right changes into a moral wrong? It might be placed at the point where personal feeling denies to others the right to earn a living; it becomes a social menace where a concerted understanding saddles onto a class a burden of economic disability.

* * *

After this general circling over the employment field, let us now become as specific as possible and attempt to judge just how strict the exclusion is, and where it may be found.

Office work as a class is difficult for Jews to obtain. Something of the law of supply and demand operates here, for the commercial schools prepare

Jewish boys and girls by tens of thousands for clerkships of one sort and another. Most offices do not want them. This statement is supported by personal investigation, the reports of job-seekers, surveys, and the testimony of the agencies both commercial and non-profit, Jewish, and non-sectarian. Estimates are approximate, of course, but they are based upon first-hand information and usually from non-Jewish sources. The figures which at first glance appear most extreme are the ones from persons in position to know most accurately. Such a statement, scarcely credible but soundly backed by conservative and informed observers, is this:

IN GENERAL OFFICE WORK, ABOUT NINETY PERCENT OF THE JOBS AVAILABLE IN NEW YORK ARE BARRED TO JEWS.

This does not mean that only ten percent of the office jobs are held by Jews. In spite of bans and quotas, Jews get in. For a variety of personal reasons, they obtain places. But it does mean that walking in cold to the employment market, an average Jew finds that nine out of ten of the jobs otherwise possible to him, and for which a Gentile would have a chance, are entirely beyond his reach. And the reason is that he is a Jew.

Except for the increased unemployment since the panic of 1929, discrimination is not much worse now than for the last three or four years. But there has been a steady solidification of classes in recent years, as among Jews, Catholics, Protestants, and what the agencies group as Italians and foreigners. One great cause, next to Mr. Ford's hymns of hate, was the bitterness of the 1928 Presidential campaign with its raising of the religious issue against Governor Smith. About that time came an increased tendency for Protestant firms not to employ Catholics; with Catholic firms slapping back. Jews suffered slightly and indirectly from this increased class-consciousness of the others.

One experienced agent estimated that along with the ninety percent ban on Jews, about twenty-five percent of the office jobs in New York were barred to Catholics, about eighty percent to Italians and foreigners, and about five percent to Protestants. In the single classification of stenographers, he estimated that all bans were relaxed, being slightly less than ninety percent against Jews, ten to fifteen percent to Catholics, seventy-five percent to Italians and almost none to Protestants. These figures as to non-Jews probably are considerably too high, but they indicate one informed point of view. Whereas anti-Jewish prejudice is not religious but racial and social, anti-Catholic is pointed against an immigrant background—Irish or Italian—and also against that religion.

The effect of exclusion induces a rigid sifting of the Jews who do find places, greatly to the advantage of offices which employ them. With so many refusing, the others have their pick of the highest types of Jewish help. They are able to obtain relatively greater efficiency than if they selected from the more popular classification. Hence, perhaps, has been developed part of the Jewish reputation for superior keenness. Still another angle of this problem is the frequent unfair necessity for Jewish workers to accept reduced salaries.

One of the more pointed ironies of the job boycott is the exclusion of the race of money-lenders from banking, their own ancient field, to which for centuries they were restricted by sneering and more-righteous Christians. Difficult as it is for almost anyone to get a job in a bank, it is harder by tenfold for Jews. The routine for any applicant is first to obtain a personal interview with one of the bank's employment staff, and then if considered favorably he or she is permitted to fill out an application blank and give references. These names are combed thoroughly; the applicant is checked as to religion and home life, inquiries are made of his minister, high school principal, and family physician. If this search discloses no flaw or taint, the applicant is given a medical examination, finger printed, photographed and bonded. Then when a vacancy occurs, he is put to work. The banks know when they are getting a Jew, and they keep the figure down to exactly the number desired.

The largest and richest banks in New York have rules against employing any Jews, except in unusual cases. Men familiar with downtown conditions estimate that only ten percent of the banks take Jews, and even these prefer not to; ninety percent will have none. About five percent of the banks do not take Catholics, this number including one of the largest banks of all; and thirty percent express a preference for Protestants only, but will break the rule in favor of particularly desirable Catholics.

The Manufacturers Trust Company and the Public National Bank are among the leading banks largely owned and controlled by Jews. The recently defunct Bank of United States was in the same class. Such banks have a more liberal policy toward employing Jews. However, they insist upon having a high percentage of Gentiles visible in their tellers' cages and upon their floors.

The personal testimony of a young Jewish college man of three years experience in banking is illuminating, even though one discounts it somewhat as prejudiced and *ex parte*. The quotations are from an affidavit which he made and signed January 31, 1930.

He tells of having been delayed in hearing from an application for a position as teller in a bank on the East Side. So he asked a woman in an employment agency to inquire of the cashier about him. "She told me that his answer was that because of my religion he could not use me." He then applied to a branch of the same bank in the garment section, again a Jewish neighborhood, and was advised by an official that "he was keeping a fifty-fifty ratio, half Jews and half Christians, and if he took me on it would break up the schedule."

Then the applicant gave this summary: "I have gone to the National City Bank, the Bank of Manhattan, the Corn Exchange Bank, the Chase National Bank, and the first thing they ask is 'What is your religion?' and when I tell them I am Jewish, the interview comes to an end."

It is Wall Street gossip that the exclusion of Jews there dates back to the long-ago rivalry between the two leading private banking houses in the district, when Kuhn, Loeb & Co. and J. P. Morgan & Co. were rivals in a more narrow field. This resentment of the old Gentile financial houses may be due to dread of increased competition or to distrust of what they consider untried and adventurous newcomers. But it is true that the implausible story of a great plot of Gentile financiers is dusted off whenever a Jewish institution is in difficulty.

The New York Stock Exchange employs some Jews. It is said in Wall Street that an unwritten understanding of the exchange is that a majority of its membership always must be Gentile—that not more than forty-nine percent of its members may ever be Jews. Among stock brokerage firms racial lines on employes conform largely to the customers served. In general, about sixty percent of the houses are reported as taking no Jews, fifteen percent prefer Jews and twenty-five percent express no preferences.

Insurance companies rather notoriously pay small salaries to clerical help. For this reason it might be supposed that they would be forced to accept the less-desirable applicants who were rejected by the higher-paying concerns. The insurance companies, however, as one experienced informant said, "pay everything but money." They make their positions attractive by providing lunch, short hours, insurance policies and a general paternalistic big-family system. Most of the leading companies have quotas for Jewish employes. One woman agency manager remarked that "No one has ever been able to find a time when the Metropolitan's quota was not reported already full." About ninety percent of the insurance companies notify the agencies not to send Jewish applicants for positions, and half the jobs are reported as "Protestants preferred".

Jews have turned in large numbers to certified public accountancy. It is one of the most favorable fields for them, although it now is highly congested. It is favorable because of the large number of Jewish mercantile firms. They have no objection to a man of their own race auditing their books. In smaller cities than New York where Jewish business men and auditors might meet socially, however, there is often a natural desire not to deal with accountants of the same race.

The great corporations whose stocks constitute the blue chips of the Stock Exchange are for the most part unfavorable. Jewish applicants for work are not sent to them. At the same time, virtually all make a "front". If the charge of discrimination is ever made, they may say truly, "Why there is Mr. Solomon right over there."

The New York Telephone Company is one of those mentioned first by Jews in discussing companies which practice exclusion. "They don't take Jews," is the phrase. "I know a Jewish girl who works there," said one social worker. "She told them her name was McCarthy." Agencies favorable to Jews advise them not to apply.

But officials of the company, when asked, denied the charge flatly. They have no question as to race or religion on their application blank, say they do not know how many Jews there are, but do know some in all departments. There are Jews in rather high executive and technical positions with the company. Representatives of the employment office go recruiting for prospective operators to the schools of the East Side where the Jewish population is predominant.

However, company officials do say that a considerable number of Jewish girls eliminate themselves. After the conditions of the work are explained to them, with a clear statement of the requirement for service on the holidays as usual, many do not file their blanks. Also, they say, the element of diction being highly important in a telephone operator, many Jewish girls from immigrant homes are rejected for their accent.

The public utility companies as a class, largely in control of Gentiles and representing monopolies against which the Jews could not hope to make effective retaliation, are considered the hardest fields of all for Jews to enter. Some of them are said bluntly to have a one hundred percent ban on Jewish employes. The question of religion enters here in odd fashion. One or two of the companies have a policy of All-Protestant control and succession but take care to divide Protestant and Catholic employes half and half. This makes for smooth diplomatic relations with the strongly Catholic Tammany Hall, the political overlord by whose favor the company exists.

Some of the old and exclusive stores on Fifth Avenue are strongholds against Jews in the merchandise field. There are stores who employ no Jews, or almost none, at all. Virtually all have quotas, and one personnel specialist familiar with the whole field estimated that the department store most liberal toward Jews would not take them in greater number than thirty percent of their total. The same expert reported that not one large store had an employment manager who was a Jew.

The discrimination against Jews is relaxed in the higher executive positions, among buyers, and in some of the advertising departments. They are considered particularly good buyers. In stores which have a strict general policy against Jews, some get in through the influence of a Jewish buyer who makes a pointed recommendation to the sales department head.

Jewish applicants of the better type have been helped, generally, by the recent policy of stores to seek college girls for sales positions. For the better positions, it is said, type counts for more than race. Smart shops are coming to give a chance to a Jewish girl if she is well-educated, pleasant-mannered, good-looking, and tall.

The foregoing statements, while from authoritative sources, do not come from store executives, of course. No store would make any public utterance to offend a single one of the accounts of wealthy Jewish customers, who are sought after. For this reason, in recruiting salesgirls of non-Jewish type, the stores often turn the assignment over confidentially to employment agencies, who may take the blame for rejecting Jewish applicants.

One of the largest low-priced chain store organizations in the world, which employs hundreds of Jewish girls at minimum salaries as salesgirls, has an ironclad rule against taking Jews into their general offices in New York.

A Jew, Bernard Lichtenberg, is president of the Association of National Advertisers. In a recent interview in the *Jewish Tribune* he remarked that few Jews were active in advertising, only six or seven that he could think of holding outstanding positions. There are bars against Jews, and some advertising agencies in New York refuse them. He said:

> "There is a reluctance to employ Jews as beginners, but given sufficient ability, sufficient persistence and the qualities of character necessary for success, these bars can be broken down. Outstanding ability is always recognized. . . .
>
> "Any organization will accept a Jew as a partner or as a chief executive, for by the time he has reached that point, he is too good for them to care whether he is Jewish or not. But at the same time they may not be inclined to give a start to young and untried Jews. . . .
>
> "The question of personality, racial and individual, and a natural inclination for

> one's own race in preference to others enters here. One trouble is that an unpleasant Jew is not looked upon as a terrible specimen of humanity, but as a terrible specimen of the Jewish race."

In editorial departments of newspapers one may observe men who have not been barred from the very topmost and most desirable positions by the fact that they were Jews. Quoting the *Jewish Tribune* again, a recent article by an anonymous newspaper man concerning his experiences, said:

> "Indeed, I think that the record of the newspaper world as a whole is much freer from the taint of prejudice than possibly any other field." He encountered some prejudice, of course, but he thought, "When I met an editor face to face, it did not require any arguments on my part to prove to him that I was not more offensive than his Baptist or Episcopalian reporter. But where I had to apply by letter, as soon as I put the word 'Jew' down on paper, my lot was doomed."

Gentile newspapermen generally would agree with this estimate. There are not an overwhelming number of Jews in newspaper work, but one's personal knowledge would deny that they have been unfairly excluded. However, in almost any office in America it could happen that a managing editor, observing a chance handful of Jewish reporters clustered around a desk might say, "Well, it looks as if we had nothing but Jews on this staff. We won't hire any more for a while."

Among the more expensive chain restaurants, it is the practice to employ few Jewish waitresses, virtually no Jewish headwaitresses. Some chains confine Jewish waitresses to restaurants in districts predominantly Jewish. Even in such sections, managers have reported that Jewish customers prefer to be served by Gentile waitresses. One chain of lunch counters has the obvious slogan, "Strictly American."

In the traditional Jewish business of clothing manufacture—Jewish so much that lordly youngsters refuse to continue there in their fathers' footsteps—there are shops which do not take Jews, on a strict racial classification. This statement implies less discrimination than at first appears. The Amalgamated Clothing Workers of America have a membership in New York between sixty and seventy per cent Jewish; the greater part of the remainder, Italian. In many of the Jewish shops, only Yiddish is spoken, and none but Jews are employed. In other shops the prevailing language is Italian, and the foreman takes no Jews.

The field of union labor is far too complicated, of course, for consideration in such a survey as this. The voice of complaint, however, is likewise raised there. A recent charge of prejudice was made by Jewish members, numbering about six hundred out of a total of one thousand and seven hundred, of a Brooklyn local in the building trade. They charged that unemployment among Jewish members was entirely out of proportion to that distributed among the general membership. The assignment of men to available jobs was in the hands of the business manager, and it was charged that he deliberately overlooked the Jewish members. It is a typical complaint.

Another form of the charge of discrimination is that Jewish applicants for membership cards are unfairly excluded. The unions in the better-paid trades are closed corporations, and they have no desire to share their privileges too widely or to increase competition for themselves. One ground for this discrimination is given in a repetition of the old statement that Jews are not docile workers. They are more than usually inclined to speak out in meetings, to demand accountings from the business agent, to complain at methods of fixing and inside politics. The painters' union in New York, with a membership thirty-five percent Jewish, is considered the most favorable of the building trades, and this because of influential Jewish members who hold leading positions in the union. Opportunities for Jewish workers are much smaller in the bricklayers, electrical workers, and steamfitters unions.

* * *

Attempting a general summary of employment conditions for Jews in New York, it may be said:

Jews encounter more handicaps downtown than uptown.

Jewish women seem to have a slightly harder time than men.

Highly distinctive Jewish names are a disadvantage compared with those which are non-committal. That is, names such as Aaronson, Weinberger, Lipshutz, Levinsky or Cohen fall more harshly upon the ears of employers than Schmidt, Wise, Meyer, and Schwab, or Jones, and Van Rensselaer. By the same token, German-descended Gentiles who have names such as Schmidt, Wise, Meyer, and Schwab tell of being kept waiting until they establish that their names mean no harm and they are free from Jewish association.

As to types of work, as a general classification, and begging allowance for many exceptions, it may be said that Jews in New York have more difficulty in obtaining secretarial and stenographic work, dictaphone operation, positions with public utilities, railroads, banks, insurance companies, lawyers' offices, brokerage houses, the New York Stock Exchange, hotels, department store salesmanship, book publishing, except in the case of Jewish firms, aviation, and, as a whole, in the home offices of large corporations of the first rank.

On the other hand, lines of work comparatively easier for Jews to enter are: garment and fur trades, the textile lines, markets, provisions, commission merchants, certified public accounting, manufacturing, moving pictures and theatres, retail stores dealing in drugs, tobacco, radio, jewelry and the like, specialty shops and restaurants (although not Childs and Schraffts).

The employment field in New York reeks with prejudice. The amazing extent and bitterness of the discrimination has been confirmed by experts engaged daily in watching the field.

"I should have thought before I looked at this angle of the problem specifically that only about sixty or seventy percent of the jobs were closed to Jews," said one of these anonymous sources, who nevertheless is an experienced agency manager. "I am surprised, but I find that ninety to ninety-five percent exclusion is correct."

The Jew out of work who is looking for a job in New York faces odds of about ten to one against him.

Chapter VIII

RESTRICTED

THE typical Jewish story of exclusion from a hotel follows one familiar pattern and has been repeated ten thousand times. Mr. Rabinowitz telegraphs some pretentious out-of-town hotel for reservations. Right away comes an answering wire: "Sorry. No space available at present. All filled up." So Mr. Rabinowitz gets his Negro chauffeur or his secretary, or his brother-in-law, anybody whose name happens to be Johnson, to send exactly the same kind of request for reservation to the same hotel. Just as quickly as before comes the wire: "Rooms reserved. Many thanks." And then Mr. Rabinowitz explodes with righteous indignation.

He begins to feel almost identified with that worthy Jewish couple, Mary and Joseph, who were told there was no room for them in the inn at Bethlehem. He wonders if this is a free country or not. He fumes at the advertisement in the papers of "New York's Modern Christian Mausoleum", the new Westchester Memorial at Hastings-on-Hudson, which will not accept Jews even after they are dead. Clearly, there ought to be a law about it. And most of all, Mr. Rabinowitz thinks about those mighty men of the good old days, Isaac Seligman and Nathan Straus.

Two generations ago when Mr. Seligman was refused admission to a hotel at Saratoga Springs, New York, he turned around and built for himself nearby another hotel, the largest, then, in the world. Likewise Mr. Straus, excluded from a hotel at Lakewood, New Jersey, although his servants were offered rooms, proceeded to build the imposing Laurel-in-the-Pines, where no question of race should ever be raised. He converted it into an almost exclusively Jewish resort.

As a matter of fact, there is a law about it to a certain extent. It is an amendment to the New York Civil Rights Law, enacted in 1913, and makes it punishable as a misdemeanor for any hotel to advertise that any person is not admitted or encouraged because of race, creed or color. Some other states have a similar law. It used to be that many New Jersey hotels on their advertising matter carried the discreet line saying, "The patronage of Hebrews is not solicited."

One Jewish acquaintance told of how it felt to run into that. He had gone down to Asbury Park ten or fifteen years ago to a convention of the American Library Association. He was admitted, of course, under the general reservation made for the convention. But when he saw that line on cards around the hotel, he felt so uncomfortable that he packed up his bags and walked down the street to the next hotel. There he found the same policy. On he went to a third. As he stepped into the lobby he called out to the clerk at the desk, "Say, do you take Jews?" "Yes," said the clerk. Our librarian dropped his bags with relief, shouting, "Then you can have me."

* * *

Although the Lake Placid Club in the Adirondacks conforms strictly to the law against advertising its exclusion of Jews, it receives a generous portion of free advertising just on that point every now and then, and has never denied that it does exclude. In the fall of 1930 there was an uproar over the club when it was suggested that state money was to be expended upon its property—improving an anti-semitic institution at public cost—in preparation for the winter sports of the Olympic Games. The first outcry against the club was heard in 1905. At that time the founder and still the proprietor of the club, Dr. Melvil Dewey, inventor of the Dewey classification system for libraries and advocate of simplified spelling, was state librarian of New York. A protest was made by prominent Jews against advertising matter then legally circulated by the club over Dr. Dewey's signature, and after his removal had been requested, he resigned his state position. The circular complained of contained the statement:

> "No one will be received against whom there is physical, moral, social or race objections, or who would be unwelcome to even a small minority. This excludes absolutely all consumptives or other invalids, whose presence might injure health or modify others' freedom or enjoyment. This invariable rule is rigidly enforced. It is found impracticable to make exceptions for Hebrews or others excluded, even when of unusual personal qualifications."

Another incident involving a semi-commercial club in New York was that centering at the Westchester Biltmore Country Club in 1926, the club then being associated with the Bowman chain of hotels, but since sold and its name changed to the Westchester Country Club. There was a widespread report that Jews were not admitted to the club, in spite of the fact of its having more than two dozen Jewish members on its roster including such well-known names as Rothschild, Lehman, Benjamin, and Warburg. The original announcement of the club's formation had said, "The class of patrons will be most select." Then with theatrical furore, in May, 1926, came the announcement that Al Jolson, the actor, had resigned because of the exclusion on religious grounds of his friend, Harry Richman. His report was that an official of the club, objecting to his guest on the golf course, had told him, "If you want it straight, and you have asked for it, I am going to tell you. We don't want any Jews here." However, the other Jewish members remained, others joined, and the club continued.

The story of restriction in the United States is made up of incidents of this sort. They may be found from Lake Placid to the Royal Poinciana Hotel at Palm Beach, and out into the Rocky Mountains. Alongside most of the hotels which do not accept Jews are others which do. Occasionally a weary motorist with wife and children in a disabled car in the rain is turned away by some stupid innkeeper and forced to travel on far to find shelter. Such stories are not fictitious; likewise such extremes are not very frequent. A letter from the Adirondacks tells of certain hotels which refuse Jews unconditionally, others which admit them freely, still others which admit them grudgingly, but "they do not cater to them and in case of applicants, they are given undesirable rooms during their stay and are apt to be annoyed by not being shown the comforts and privileges given to the other guests."

From Miami, Florida, a letter dated January 20, 1930, answering a question as to anti-Jewish discrimination, reported:

"The finest hotels at Miami Beach do

not accept Jews. Mr. Adolph S. Ochs is the only one who was ever admitted."

At the same time Miami newspapers were carrying advertisements of apartments at Miami Beach with the note in parenthesis, "Gentiles only".

A resort hotel in the Pennsylvania mountains advertised, "Altitude one thousand feet; too high for Jews." "Michigan's finest resort hotel" at Charlevoix on Lake Michigan, advertised "Gentile clientele". A hotel at Toronto posted conspicuously on a signboard "A Statement of Policy" in which it asked Jews to respect its desire for none but Gentile guests; and reports of hostility to Jews may be had at the travel agencies concerning resorts as widely scattered as Hot Springs, Arkansas, and Bermuda. Many hotels on the travel agency calendars, in fact, bear the notation, "Hebrews not admitted."

But the Jewish race has been kicked out of places so much finer and larger than American hotels that the restriction sporadically practiced in this country amounts to no more than a momentary irritation. All the Jews in England were put out in the thirteenth century and did not get back, except in a sort of bootleg guise, until the time of Oliver Cromwell. They were excluded from Spain and France. One of the earliest exclusions was from the city of Kieff in Russia, in the year 1111. The historic old town of Frankfort-on-the-Main, early in the sixteenth century, enforced the exclusion of Jews from within sight or sound of the cathedral, and when Napoleon entered the city as a conqueror three centuries later he found, and had removed, a sign on the promenade which said, "Jews and Dogs Not Allowed Here."

The spirit of exclusion flared up to unusual violence in the fall of 1928 and again in 1929 in the burning of a colony of lakeshore cottages near Milwaukee. The second incident provoked from the *Milwaukee Journal* an editorial which both tells the story and represents enlightened non-Jewish opinion. It said:

> "LISTEN, GENTILE!
>
> "The Jewish owner of a group of cottages at Pewaukee Lake received an anonymous letter. It read:
>
> "'Listen, Jew! We noticed that you are again trying to rent your cottages to the same —— you had last summer. We'll murder you and all the rest like ducks, if you move in again. Remember, this is not a threat, we'll do it.'
>
> "Then, on Thursday, the ten cottages on Rocky Point were destroyed by an incendiary fire. They were burned to the ground. And neighbors, or people from Pewaukee, or passersby from somewhere

else, looted them of their furnishings and left nothing for the Jew. He was stripped of his buildings and possessions.

"It now is time for the state of Wisconsin to write a letter. It should read like this: 'Listen, Gentile! Moved by the lowest form of race prejudice, you have practiced an outrageous persecution upon a citizen of this state. You have stepped from the levels of decency, fair play and tolerance to the level of a coward, acting by stealth like a rat. Moreover you have broken the laws against arson. For that the state fire marshal now is charged to assemble at Pewaukee any force of men that may be necessary to get you; any force of detectives needed to ferret you out as other rats are routed out, if it takes a special appropriation by act of legislature to do it.

" 'And the fire marshal is charged to take you into the courts and there, by fair trial, get you convicted and sentenced to the state prison at Waupun for as long a term as the laws and the judge may decree for an act so despicable as this. And if, by proper evidence, it can be established who helped to persecute and loot the Jew, in the state of Wisconsin in this year of

> enlightenment, 1929, then every one—neighbor, resident of Pewaukee, or passer-by—will be punished to the full extent of the law so that this shame upon the state may be wiped as clean as such a smudge ever can be wiped. This is the word of the decent people of Wisconsin who, as Americans, acknowledge no intolerance and practice no persecutions against any creed or faith or sect.' "

* * *

New York City with its huge Jewish population attempts to exclude Jews from buildings just as do other cities of the United States. There are office buildings in Wall Street, Broadway, and elsewhere downtown, which do not rent to Jews. There are restrictions even in buildings owned by Jews themselves. Real estate offices abound in jokes about Jews who cannot live under their own roofs.

This form of discrimination, for many years so striking and so widespread, is the one which appears today most likely to fade out. The change has been brought about principally by money pressure, which has aided the boldness of certain Jewish operators and building contractors. With the tremendous, feverish activity in construction of high-priced apartment buildings in New York came a need to rent them without delay. Exclusion of Jews kept off the prospect list a great class of moneyed people who desired pretentious living quarters. Facing this condition, builders frankly defied neighborhood tradition and rented to whomsoever had the price.

In the face of the tidal wave of Jewish immigration from Europe, and of the later waves of Jews rapidly acquiring wealth and social ambitions, the old New York has given ground grudgingly and always with a struggle. In the 1860's, 70's and 80's, the principal property owner on Second Avenue would not rent to Jews. Far Rockaway later had clubs and hotels which refused to admit Jews, and there were no Jews in the Bay Ridge section of Brooklyn. All those regions today have become predominantly Jewish in population, and there are many others with similar history.

The spread of Jewish residence in New York City has followed somewhat the same pattern as the course of an individual family which rises progressively in social and financial status.

Beginning with residence in the East Side, the family first moves to the Bronx or certain sections of Harlem or Brooklyn. The next step might be to Washington Heights, then to Riverside Drive or West End Avenue, next to Fifth Avenue or Park Avenue, finally to the ultimate goal of social progress, an estate in the more exclusive sections of Westchester County.

Along all this course there have been obstacles such as in the still-existing restricted section in Fieldston, and many others in and around the city, yet the tension is strongest in Fifth and Park Avenues.

Riding on a Fifth Avenue bus in New York, one may notice advertisements of the desirable residential development in Jackson Heights: "Restrictions, Convenience, Service." At the renting office, one inquires, "What about restrictions?" "Oh, yes," says the agent, "It's one hundred percent restricted." "What does that mean—no Jews?" "That's right. We don't take any Jews at all. Our people have moved in under that condition, and we've got to protect them."

A Jewish family, personal acquaintances, coming to New York, thought they would settle in Bronxville on account of the exceptionally good public school for their two children. "But," said some of their informed friends, "you can't live in Bronxville. The children will be miserable because they are Jewish." The mother went back to make inquiries of the teacher at school. "I don't think the matter ever came up," said the teacher, "but I'll inquire. I hope you will come, though." Then later the teacher reported, "Yes, I hear there is rather strong prejudice and it might be disagreeable. But I'd be glad to have you try." They did not take the chance.

House hunting in an outlying moderate-priced residence section in the summer of 1930, the wife of another friend, not Jewish, was being shown apartments. The agent volunteered:

"You'll find this a very desirable, highly restricted neighborhood. We've got a high class of people here—no Italians, no Negroes, and no Jews! Of course, now and then a Jew does slip in on us." He named a well-known actor. "Now that fellow. He got his wife's mother to rent a place for him, and we couldn't help that. We didn't know who she was doing it for, otherwise he couldn't have got it."

Then reassuringly, he added, "But he's four or five blocks away from here."

Representatives of a seashore real estate development on Long Island in the spring of 1930 had an advertising exhibit in the lobby of a large New York hotel. The question was put frankly to this company's agent. "If I were a Jew, would you sell me a lot?"

"I should say not," was the answer. "None of them gets in here. I simply tell them the section is restricted and we can't sell. But even if they managed to get a lot and build there, it wouldn't do any good. They would be ostracized and excluded from any enjoyment of the place. There is a community club which controls the beach and all social affairs, and they never would get into the club. They'd be glad enough to sell out and move away."

Restrictions are not confined to the new or moderate priced residence colonies. The most iron clad and copper bottomed exclusion around New York, reputedly, exists in that stronghold of wealth and fashion, Tuxedo Park. "Any Jews there?" a real estate man was asked.

"Not if Tuxedo Park knows it," he answered.

* * *

Park Avenue is the scene of the story frequently repeated of a Gentile of wealth who had married a Jewess. After several years residence in an apartment, he was asked by the superintendent to move out. Why? Because his small children, going in and out of the building with their nurse, "looked too Jewish."

Park Avenue also is the setting for that other anecdote about the prosperous Jew who goes to the building manager and asks the price of an apartment. "I'm sorry, Sir, but I can't quote you the figure because none are available just now," he is told.

The Jew persists. What are prices, anyhow? When will one be available? Why can't he get some information?

"Well, since I have to," says the manager, "I am forced to tell you that it is simply against our policy to take in any Jews."

"Oh, pardon me," answers the Jew. "I didn't get you at first. I didn't mean to suggest, of course, that I was good enough to live here. But the fact is, I am keeping a blonde in this building, and I was just checking up to see if she is gypping me on what she said was the rent charge."

Park Avenue is the battle ground in New York, Fifth Avenue is holding out a little harder, and the newer developments along the East River, such as Beekman and Sutton Places and Carl Schurz Park represent the virtually unassailed citadels of old New York Gentile society. In other parts of the city and at lower rentals, there are also certain apartments and areas which do not admit Jews, as well as certain real estate operators who refuse to deal with them. Before the War, conditions were different. Jews were excluded almost without exception from upper Fifth Avenue. The fashionable Park Avenue apartments on New York Central property north of the Grand Central Station would not rent to a Jew. But the pressure of population and the strain of rising real estate values was too great. Within the single month of May, 1925, the Jewish real estate speculator, Benjamin Winter, bought the famous chateau of Mrs. W. K. Vanderbilt at Fifth Avenue and Fifty-second Street and the mansion of Vincent Astor at Fifth Avenue and Sixty-fifth Street. As if to make the change more emphatic, he turned the site of the latter over to his co-religionists for the erection of Temple Emanu-El.

Jews today are among the most active and prominent figures in the New York real estate field. Of the actual equities, one informed operator estimated that Jews own about forty percent of the city real estate, which is not much more than their share according to population. But he figured that they make up eighty percent of the speculative and operating group and are almost equally dominant in construction. But in building management, at least eighty percent are Christians.

A large Jewish operator in conversation frankly asserted that exclusion in some of the present anti-Jewish strongholds is supported by the banks. Without the evidence of an actual case in point, simply to be judged on its own merit as an individual's statement, his remark was:

"If anyone evaded or violated the understanding, renewal of his mortgage would be refused or, at best, it would be made very difficult for him. If he persisted in trying to get a new mortgage, appraisals would be made so low that he might find it impossible. This may not be legal or constitutional. But it is an effective bludgeon."

The banks in apparently punishing an operator for letting in Jews might be acting from mere spite and prejudice, or they might possibly be recognizing an economic factor of importance. If the admission of Jews to an apartment made that building less desirable in the eyes of the public, the banks might argue, then the building becomes a poorer security. So, under some circumstances, the bank might foreclose on the owner who dared take Jews into his building.

Yet the breaking of restrictions in rented apartments in Park Avenue came through the refusal of Jewish operators and builders to recognize such community agreements. Buying property which had been considered sacrosanct to Gentiles, they proceeded to fill vacancies with applicants who appeared personally acceptable, regardless of whether they were Jews or Gentiles. In some cases tenants protested, even moved out. Others waited and grew accustomed or reconciled to their new neighbors.

The case is not so clear, however, concerning all Jewish property owners. Just as Jewish employers frequently refuse to take workers from their own race, so Jewish owners and real estate agents often are accused of discrimination in rentals. One Jewish agent who was upbraided by his fellows for the exclusion policy of his concern, made the sweeping explanation that he represented a group of owners almost entirely Jewish, and they would not permit him to rent to Jews.

On Fifth and Park Avenues, the zone of extreme restriction extends roughly from Fifty-ninth Street to Eighty-sixth Street. This is the home of the most expensive cooperative apartments, and the cooperative represents the peak of inventiveness to date in the residential ostracism movement. This area—not by chance—straddles the point fixed by the Social

Register as the social center of New York, every year determined on the basis of residence of those recognized in the Register. At present the center is in Seventieth Street, just east of Park Avenue, in a back yard. The Register is not much more liberal toward Jews than is the prevailing real estate policy of the region. The center shifted gradually north as the city developed, and swung sharply away from Fifth Avenue with the movement of social leaders to the banks of the East River.

* * *

Jews as a class have not taken to cooperatives even those of such wealth as to afford the finest quarters. For the most part, they reside in rented apartments. However, there is a notable exception in one cooperative building exclusively occupied by wealthy Jewish families in the heart of the restricted region in Park Avenue.

Cooperative apartment houses rest upon the theory of individual home ownership and congeniality of environment, even though they are constructed at a profit by development companies and sold to groups none of the members of which were previously acquainted. The real estate transactions of this section are handled by a small number of powerful firms which enforce a virtually complete exclusion at the start. After control has passed into the hands of the occupants, new admissions are protected by a blackball system as effectively as in a club. A glance at cooperative apartment advertisements in the New York Sunday newspapers, with the prevalence of such phrases as "highly restricted", "exclusive", and "choose your own neighbors" is, of itself, convincing evidence of the extent of the practice.

The fact that Jews happened to own building sites in Park Avenue considered desirable has been no obstacle to plans for constructing exclusive cooperatives there. There is one case, probably there are more, of a wealthy Jew being the only member of his race permitted in a building erected on his own lot. There is another instance of a Jewish owner of a Fifth Avenue corner who was approached by a cooperative company being organized, and himself invited to invest in the company—with the understanding that of course he should not live in the building himself. The story actually ends in his refusal.

Leasing agreements are different, and in some cases extremely specific. In Chicago, and perhaps in New York also, a tenant is sometimes bound and restricted by oral provisions supplementing the written contract. Thus it has been provided, orally, that if the landlord discovers any Jewish blood in the family, the lease shall become void; that, of course, Jewish friends may call at the apartment and even stay overnight, but that no such visit may be extended beyond ten days. Many cities have residential districts similar to Baltimore's Roland Park, practically non-Jewish but in which one or two Jews of financial and social prominence are permitted.

The cooperative system has the great advantage of avoiding all mention of the disagreeable subject of Jewish exclusion. Admission is not renting an apartment; it is joining a club. Race and religion need never be mentioned. Fitness is determined by congeniality and personality. Such an agreement is enforceable at law. Any person desiring to buy into a cooperative would be received with courtesy when he made inquiries. Both he and his wife would be inspected carefully when they came back to look the place over. With their application for space the man would be required to furnish at least three business and three personal references. While he is making up his mind about the apartment, the company is making up its mind about him.

A case of exclusion in a cooperative got into the New York papers in December, 1927, through the suit filed by the owner of a penthouse at 32 Washington Square, West, to compel her fellow-tenants to permit her to sublet to a Jew. The plaintiff said her prospective tenant was:

"A lawyer, a member of a prominent firm, married, of unimpeachable moral character, of a most genial and peaceful disposition, a very quiet and satisfactory neighbor, of excellent financial standing and a director of a trust company."

Attached to her complaint was a letter from a director of the corporation, virtually admitting her charges but giving this explanation:

> "All with whom I talked seemed to approach the question from a strictly business standpoint. No one mentioned to me any personal antipathy. The business aspect of the matter is that we all have a good sized investment in the house and all have the same interest in its financial success, and we believe that to restrict the renting against Hebrews will greatly improve the rental values which they would have in the absence of any such restriction. . . . Many people of the class of tenants to whom we must look in renting have a prejudice against close association with Hebrews, so by restricting the house in that respect we adopt a measure which will strongly appeal to many prospective tenants."

The case was settled out of court, the defendant realty corporation filing a confession of judgment admitting that it owed the owner of the penthouse the sum of $3,300 for the damages she had suffered.

The contracts for cooperatives generally provide that there shall be no assignment or sub-letting without the consent of two-thirds either of the full board of directors or of the stockholders.

* * *

Hotels in New York City, and commercial hotels in cities all over this country, are driven by a constant necessity to keep their rooms filled. They are glad to have Jewish guests. It may be said confidently that there is no discrimination in this field. There have been stories of such discrimination in the past. Yet even the bitterest of these have been denied by the hotels, and are re-told with attendant circumstances which divert the cause of exclusion from the point of race. Even in the field of resort hotels, exclusion is relaxing. In their own phrase, the hotels are "letting down the bars." The automobile has been a large factor toward liberalism here, for with its stirring up of the tourist class, making for short stops, the hotels do not have the old time all-season-long reliable guests of decades ago. They must make more concessions to transients.

One ancient practice has been almost universally abandoned. It was a custom in many hotels at Atlantic City to exclude Jews during "the season," from about Lincoln's Birthday to October. But while customers were few, and the low winter rates were in effect, they would accept them. But Atlantic City is a year-round resort for Jews today.

Still, the travel bureaus report many resort hotels, including those operated by Jews, as being cautious about wholesale Jewish trade. The proprietors say they desire to pick their own guests, individually. Others repeat the old phrase, "Don't send me any kikes."

That brings up the question of definition. The proverb of the race has it that "a kike is the Jew who has just left the room." In the mind of the hotel proprietor, it doubtless means the reverse of what he calls "nice-looking Jewish people." Even if the Jew escapes the designation of kike, there remains for him the old and bitter struggle—in finding home and shelter as everywhere else—with the burden of being simply Jewish.

Chapter IX

"INSULT TO INJURY"

THEODORE ROOSEVELT's appointment of Oscar S. Straus to be Secretary of Commerce and Labor in 1906, ten years before Louis D. Brandeis was placed on the Supreme Court, was a triumphant event for all the Jews in America. No other member of their race ever had sat in the President's cabinet. It contributed its share to the general popularity of the President with this particular group.

Five years later at the council meeting of the Union of American Hebrew Congregations it was arranged to have both Colonel Roosevelt and Mr. Straus present at a banquet given at the Astor Hotel in New York, on Wednesday night, January 18, 1911. The leading members of the Jewish community were present. The former President, being much in demand, did not arrive until the banquet was far advanced and the speeches in progress.

When he spoke, Colonel Roosevelt paid a personal tribute to his friend, Oscar Straus. He said—as any other politician might have done—that in appointing him to his cabinet he had not been moved by political considerations or a desire to cultivate any powerful minority group, but that he had sought simply the best possible man, whether Jew or Gentile.

At this, the large company did a strange thing. They burst into unwilling but unsuppressed laughter, and a look of surprise came over the speaker's face. The reason was that before Colonel Roosevelt arrived, the toastmaster had introduced the patriarchal Jacob H. Schiff. And during his remarks, Mr. Schiff had let slip this information:

"While we are honoring Mr. Straus, I am proud to say that I had a part in his selection. The President sent for me and said, 'I want to put a Jew in my cabinet. Who is the best one I can get?' And I said, 'You should name Oscar Straus.' "

Operating for either honor or insult, advantage or disadvantage, the recognition of a Jew's Jewishness is constantly present in America today. It may be disclaimed but it is never overlooked, is always accented, and is becoming more clearly outstanding. This wall cuts across the entire structure of activity, affecting Jews at work and on their holidays, in their homes and clubs, and in public life, in education, worship, reputation, and all the contacts and competitions which make up the social ferment of normal, non-ascetic existence. Not all these separations are of equal importance, and they do not affect equally the entire Jewish group. The wealthy Jew may be injured most deeply by the prejudice which rejects him from a club, and at this discrimination his lowly brother may be inclined to a malicious laugh. The latter has suffered more intimately; he has been refused a chance to earn his living, because he was a Jew, and possibly his rejection from a job came from the very same comfortable compatriot who has been hurt in his social aspirations. But in small concerns as well as large, for the rich as for the poor, prejudice operates constantly as a handicap and a constraint.

* * *

In politics the classification—if you prefer that word to prejudice—on the ground of Jewishness is a definite factor which no precinct captain or district leader can be so stupid as to ignore. Any group which embraces one-third of the votes in New York City may expect to be wooed; likewise, any minority group may expect to encounter limitations. This is practical politics, if you will. It is also discrimination.

The use of racial tags in politics, attempted often by Jews as well as non-Jews when they happen to be in position to benefit, is not encouraged by the more thoughtful leaders of either class. The late Louis Marshall wrote to the secretary of a "Hebrew" Democratic club in 1927, saying, "You are playing with fire and with edged tools. The idea of getting political recognition because one is a Jew is, to me, unspeakably shameful. . . . There is no Hebrew vote."

Gerrymandering may exist to the disadvantage of Jewish sections, and a map of New York City according to assembly districts certainly is an oddly jigsawed puzzle. Again, however, such manipulation would be simply practical politics. With Tammany so dominant as it has been of recent years, the organization is able to name about whomsoever it chooses. In the strongly Jewish districts, it seems to be the policy to nominate a Jew as either an alderman or an assemblyman, but rarely both.

Of the sixty-five members of the board of aldermen for 1930-31 seven were Jewish; at least twice that number of assemblymen from the city were Jewish. Four of the city's twenty-four congressmen were Jewish. Only one of these is from Brooklyn, the most strongly Jewish borough. The office of Borough President of Manhattan has come to be regarded as virtually a Jewish birthright. But it is in the selection of judges that the political aspirations of Jews attain the warmest satisfaction. Whether this reflects the large number of Jewish lawyers in practice or not, it is true that the most ardent pleader would have little to complain of in counting the Jewish judges of the various courts in Manhattan.

In voting, the Jewish precincts give excessive majorities to their own candidates; the non-Jewish precincts, vice versa. The Jewish vote and the non-Jewish vote, however, both are such variable qualities as to be difficult for mathematical calculation.

When Oscar S. Straus was a candidate for governor on the "Bull Moose" ticket in 1912, he received two thousand more votes in the whole state than did Roosevelt for President. In the state election of 1928 the Democrats nominated Col. Herbert H. Lehman for lieutenant governor, and the Republicans, Albert Ottinger for governor, both Jews. Studying the vote, one finds that Col. Lehman, who was elected, ran fifty thousand votes behind Governor Roosevelt and five thousand behind Senator Copeland, his party-mates who also won. Governor Smith, the democratic nominee for President, did not carry the state but he received ten thousand more votes than Col. Lehman. Ottinger, the Jew, led the Republican ticket, except for President Hoover. The lesson would seem to be that there is little in race as compared with personality.

However, if one wishes to read anti-Jewish discrimination into the returns, he may point out that in the whole state exclusive of the five strongly Jewish counties in New York City, Ottinger trailed the ticket, receiving thirty-five thousand votes fewer than the Republican nominee for lieutenant governor and twenty-five thousand fewer than the nominee for the senate.

In casting about to explain Governor Smith's surprising loss of New York in his race for president in 1928, political critics have discussed the possibility that the Irish-dominated Tammany organization knifed him in reprisal for his friendship toward Jews. There was resentment, according to the story, because of his favoritism for Mrs. Moskowitz, Judge Proskauer, and others. Although well-informed Jews and non-Jews alike had heard the story, none could be found in the course of a rather faithful inquiry who believed it.

Two members of Congress upon the floor of the House recently made separate charges of discrimination against Jews in different branches of the government service. Representative LaGuardia, of Italian descent, charged that qualified Jewish applicants were rejected from appointments in the diplomatic service, while Representative Celler, a Jew, said there was discrimination against Jewish immigrants in certain parts of Eastern Europe by American consular and immigration officials.

Expanding his criticisms of the Foreign Service in a letter, Representative LaGuardia said:

> "I do not hesitate to say that there is discrimination against Jews in the Department of State.
>
> "Bright college men have no trouble in passing the examination. Then there is a so-called oral test of which no record is kept. They have some method of marking based on appearance, poise, demeanor, speech and things of that sort. I must say,

> that they really do not take measurement of the angle of the applicant's nose.
>
> "However, I am told that their ears are tuned for the broad 'A' and that the applicant's family history and connections are a part of the factors which enter into the marking in this oral test. The fact remains that few Jewish boys make the grade.
>
> "A casual glance at the roster of the Department of State, both here and abroad, confirms my charge. The most discouraging part of it all is that the rare exception who manages in one way or another to break in is the first to deny that any discrimination is made. I find these fellows to be a sort of *Toches Lechers*.
>
> "I have one particular person in mind who, because he has been invited to tea with the Third or Fourth Assistant Secretary of the Siamese Legation, thinks he is a diplomat and denies that there is any discrimination in our Foreign Service against the Jews. He happens to be Jewish but in his contact with Christians is the first to criticize his own kind."

Representative Celler charged that "intelligence tests" were used to keep out Jewish immigrants. His remarks, quoting the *Congressional Record* of January 10, 1928, were:

> "From my examination of this entire subject I am convinced that, despite assurances given by the Surgeon General, who is in Washington, and perhaps does not know exactly what is going on in Europe, these tests are deliberately used to discriminate against certain classes of aliens and against aliens particularly who are of a certain faith."

The Congressman cited as one example that twenty-three out of fifty applicants in one group at Warsaw had been turned down as mental defectives. The test by which they had been judged and disqualified included such questions as:

> "How many teeth has a crow?
>
> "How many stars are there in heaven?
>
> "What is the difference between the sky and the earth?
>
> "What is glass made of?
>
> "Which flies better, a bird or a fly?"

And so on!

Local examples of anti-Jewish feeling in politics could be collected, as of various periods, from all over the country. Maryland was the most persistent of the states in the legal sanction of prejudice. It continued until 1826 in a statute that prevented Jews from holding office or practicing law by requiring an oath of belief in the Christian religion. The law finally was repealed through the efforts of Thomas Kennedy of Hagerstown, and his famous "Jew Bill".

A story from Baltimore indicates a resumption of the spirit nearly a century later, in 1910. Then a certain Max Ways, a democratic nominee for city clerk, was defeated while all other nominees of his party were elected. Political opponents had circulated handbills advising, "Do not vote for Max Ways, the Jew." Mr. Ways, in fact, was a Catholic.

* * *

H. L. Mencken in his *Treatise on the Gods* summed up in a neat package the greater part of currently-asserted generalized antagonism to Jews in his now famous paragraph:

> "The Jews could be put down very plausibly as the most unpleasant race ever heard of. As commonly encountered they lack many of the qualities that mark the civilized man: courage, dignity, incorruptibility, ease, confidence. They have vanity without pride, voluptuousness without taste, and learning without wisdom. Their fortitude, such as it is, is wasted upon

> puerile objects, and their charity is mainly a form of display."

This is a fair sample of the slurs heaped upon the race, thousands of times in deed and publicly spoken word, millions of times in thought and intimate conversation. At the end of this road is the not-infrequent statement that Jews are a class of criminals. But before reaching that stage, there are intermediate insults.

Roget's *Thesaurus* for more than half a century, down to the latest edition, gave authority to use "Jew" as a synonym for cunning, usurer, extortioner, heretic, lickpenny, harpy, schemer, crafty, shifty, and other unpleasant words. It was the formulation of all the characteristics commonly understood as belonging to Shylock, with none of those associated with Jesus. The bad name has pursued since the hill of Golgotha. The removal of "Jew" from these lists of synonyms symbolizes a fundamental improvement of condition, or its possibility. It aims at removing from people's minds the idea that "Jewish" is somehow equivalent to evil. And it is just at that spot in the mind that prejudice has its root.

The world has not felt inhibited about frank repetition of this insult. Still, one is a little bit surprised to find today, even in a remote rural weekly such as *The Cimarron News* of Boise City, in the Panhandle region of Oklahoma, a half page garage advertisement, in letters more than an inch high, saying:

> "NALL TIRE STORES are not JEW STORES
>
> "We do not have a sale on some cheap second grade tire all the time. Etc. Etc."

The fruit of such racial irritation was pointed out by John Spargo in his book, *The Jew and American Ideals,* when he said:

"Hatred of the Jew, even when it is motivated by economic fear and resentment, will inevitably nurture every other form of anti-Semitic prejudice. If the campaign of the anti-Semites succeeds in cultivating that fear and hatred in the minds and hearts of our people, there can be no assurance against occurrence of pogroms here."

* * *

Dislike of the race, seeking to rationalize itself by the thought that Jews are an evil breed, finds expression every so often in the charge of criminality. The mouth-piece often appears to be merely a channel for the outflowing of a community sentiment. Jews themselves, on the other hand, like to remember the record that during the first century of existence of the United States, not one of their race was convicted of murder throughout the nation.

The most famous expressions of the insult in current memory have been that of then Police Commissioner Theodore A. Bingham in an article on "Foreign Criminals in New York" published in the *North American Review,* September, 1908, and that of Judge Nathan Cayton, himself a Jew, of the Municipal Court of Washington, D. C., just after Christmas, 1929.

Commissioner Bingham charged that with Jews at that time numbering about one million, or a fourth of the population of New York City, he found "perhaps half the criminals of that race." He went on to specify that "the juvenile Hebrew emulates the adult in the matter of crime percentages, forty percent of the boys at the House of Refuge and twenty-seven percent of those arraigned in the Children's Court being of that race."

The Jewish community, of course, was indignant. Figures were checked, independent investigations made, and the charges disproved—with heat. Confronted with evidence, the commissioner retracted. The very next issue of the *Review,* October, 1908, printed a letter from him saying:

> "The figures used in the article were not compiled by myself but were unfortunately assumed to be correct. It now appears, however, that these figures are unreliable. Hence it becomes my duty frankly to say so and repudiate them."

Judge Cayton repeated the charge before a synagogue congregation. He was quoted as saying:—

> "Almost overnight we have produced far more than our share of criminals. The Jewish crime wave is an actual, shameful, awful reality. I believe that during the past decade, we have definitely failed to perform our duty as Jews and Americans."

The response was quite as indignant and as prompt as it had been two decades earlier. The judge was challenged on the records.

Rabbi Abram Simon of the Washington Hebrew Synagogue cited for the judge's information the reports on federal prisons. These showed that in 1928, there were received in the Atlanta penitentiary only one hundred and forty-nine Jews out of a total of two thousand six hundred and twenty-one; at McNeil Island, twelve out of six hundred and fifty-five, and at the Chillicothe Reformatory, eleven out of four hundred and ninety. The American Jewish Committee has prepared a study of prison populations in New York City and State for the ten years up to 1925, and their conclusion is that "criminality punishable by imprisonment was less among the Jews than among persons of other births."

The New York State Commission of Correction, in its annual report published late in 1930, gives figures on the religious instruction of prisoners committed during the year ending June 30, 1929, at Auburn, Clinton, and Sing Sing. For all three prisons in a state having a heavily Jewish population the total was one hundred and thirty-eight Jews out of one thousand nine hundred and twenty-eight. The New York City penal institutions, drawing from a population nearly one-third Jewish, for the same year reported admitting ten thousand seven hundred and ninety Jewish males out of a total of fifty-nine thousand eight hundred and thirty-one, and nine hundred and ninety-three females out of ten thousand seven hundred and ninety. The violent Jew-baiter might raise the point against these figures that they meant only that Jews were too slick and devious to be caught. Whatever the true explanation, their criminal record as a racial group is pale.

The Jewish Communal Survey of Greater New York shows a marked decline in the rate of juvenile delinquency among Jews. From 1916 to 1926, it reported that not only was the Jewish juvenile delinquency rate lower than that of the general white population but it was dropping faster. It fell from 1.16 per thousand of the Jewish population in 1916 to .56 per thousand in 1926. Jewish adult delinquency, the survey reported, was not declining so rapidly. However, it decreased from 8.9 per thousand of the Jewish population in 1916 to 7.6 per thousand in 1926.

Mordecai M. Noah, when he took office years ago as sheriff of New York, heard the taunting remark, "Pity Christians who have to be hanged by a Jew." Promptly he flung back, "Pity Christians who require hanging at all."

* * *

Jews also run into the stinging annoyance of prejudice in a wide variety of other everyday experiences. They find it in clubs, of all grades from the Y.M.C.A. to that home of wealth and position, the Brook. The fact of exclusion is set down here neither in pain nor in anger, for it is the privilege of men to pick their own associates. Birds of a feather always have contrived to flock together. The observer can but report that often in such flocks the Jew discovers he is *persona non grata.*

However, a considerable number of Jews express their private resentment at such sparsely-Jewish organizations as the University Club and the Century Association by refusing to attend luncheons there or even to step with members inside the doors. A great stir was raised in the newspapers over the discovery that certain well-known and talented Jews had been kept out of the Long Shore Beach and Country Club, which was supposed to be something of a suburban community affair, at Westport, Conn.

As for the Y.M.C.A., here is a story of guaranteed reliability. The date happened fittingly to be on Rosh Hashanah, 1930. A Jew and a non-Jew decided they needed more exercise and ought to take up handball. They went to the Twenty-third Street Y.M.C.A. in New York to apply for membership. The Jew is not a strongly-accented type in his appearance. They explained that they wanted to begin handball at once, if they might; they had brought gymnasium costumes and would play that afternoon if they might join. The young man at the desk gave them application cards to fill out. Naturally, since it was a religious institution, there were questions as to religion, church membership, name of pastor and so on. The non-Jew happened to present his application first:

"All right, Sir," said the clerk. "If you will just let me have the membership fee, you may go right up to the gymnasium now." Then the Jewish applicant presented his card. The young man hesitated. "I am sorry," he said courteously, "but the rule is that men of your religion must first be interviewed by the membership secretary. I think it is because there is a percentage." The membership secretary was not in.

So the pair did not join and did not play their handball at that Y.M.C.A. The application was made really from the motive of exercise, without thought of getting data. But it happened that the non-Jewish one of the pair was one of the authors of this book.

The Y.M.C.A. conducted a questionnaire among its membership recently, concerning various points of policy. A good many replies are typified by the one from which this quotation is made: "We should limit the number of Jews. Otherwise we will drive away Protestant Christians from whom most of our support must come."

The general policy of the Y.M.C.A. in New York is to hold to a quota of five percent Jewish membership, with local branches in some sections admitting as high as twenty percent. Jews are not encouraged to live in the dormitories.

The Masonic fraternity likewise has its problems of discrimination. Certain lodges and clubs are virtually all Jewish. Others have no Jewish members, and occasional public outcry arises when such organizations express their prejudices more than their brotherhood in keeping applicants out.

Such a case was that involving the Metropolitan Masons Country Club near Briarcliff, N. Y., in December, 1927, when Supreme Court Justice Arthur S. Tompkins, a past grand master of New York State Masons, resigned explosively as both director and member of the club. His reason, he said, was because he had become convinced that there was discrimination against Jewish applicants for membership. Within a year the charge of discrimination in the ritual was raised by two women's organizations affiliated with Masonry, located a continent apart.

In the summer of 1929 the New Jersey organization of the Order of the Eastern Star was disrupted by an attempt to force upon an all-Jewish chapter a ritualistic reference to "the star of Bethlehem", while a similar attempt the following May brought threats of secession from a lodge of Job's Daughters in California.

Middletown, the famous study of a typical American city by R. S. and H. M. Lynd, published in 1929 and commonly understood to be based upon Muncie, Indiana, makes this report:

> "Racial lines, according to old residents, were less felt in the days before the Jews had come largely to dominate the retail life of the city, and before the latest incarnation of the Klan. Jewish merchants mingled freely with other business men in the smaller civic clubs, but there are no Jews in Rotary; Jews are accepted socially with just enough qualifications to make them aware that they do not entirely 'belong'."

It cannot be said that no Jews whatsoever are permitted to become members of the most pretentious and sought-after New York clubs, such as the Brook, Union, Metropolitan, Knickerbocker, University, New York Yacht or Meadow Brook. Taking the Brook as an example, however, it may be said that an examination of its membership list in the Blue Book of New York Clubs does not disclose the name of a single man of unmixed Jewish blood. A study of the lists of all the clubs mentioned fails to reveal the names of such outstanding Jews as Felix M. Warburg, Chief Justice Cardozo, Lieutenant Governor Lehman, the late Louis Marshall, or Otto H. Kahn. The men named as examples all are listed on many other club rosters, and perhaps they have never desired to join these here mentioned. Yet, except for the barrier of race, one might expect a natural affinity between such outstanding men and some such outstanding clubs.

Years ago, exclusions occurred just as now. The late Jacob A. Cantor, a state senator, first president of the Borough of Manhattan and a member of Congress, was once rejected by the then-fashionable Harlem Club. The story was told in the New York *Times* of July 10, 1889, as follows:

> "The Harlem Club which recently moved into its handsome and costly new home at Lenox Avenue and 123rd Street is disturbed by the raising of the Hebrew question. Among the invited guests at the opening reception on June 13 was Senator Jacob A. Cantor, who was prevailed on by Mr. Robert Bonynge to allow his name to

be proposed for membership. The nomination was seconded by Mr. David F. Porter. Later in the evening a member of the club who had heard of the proposal went to Senator Cantor and said: 'Jake, I have known you for a long time and I am a friend of yours, but I must tell you that in this club we draw the line at Hebrews.'

"When this speech reached the ears of Mr. George McGown, whose guest Senator Cantor was, that gentleman was naturally indignant, and he characterized it as an insult to himself. Senator Cantor went at once to Mr. Bonynge and offered to withdraw his name if he were willing, but that gentleman and the other friends of the senator had their blood up and said the senator's name should stand and be passed on if it took all summer. . . .

"There was no disguising the fact that several of the board of trustees were strongly opposed to the admission of Hebrews. Senator Cantor said the club had not yet rejected him, and, therefore, he was not in a position to discuss the matter. But he was satisfied to know that if it did reject him, it would do so on account of his race, and not on personal grounds."

Social prejudice of typically blind variety appears in the story told by a Jewish psychological consultant. A woman client, not a Jewess, during nearly a year of almost weekly professional visits to his office came to be a good friend. She told him of her husband's feeling against Jews. He had not wanted her in the first place, she said, to visit the doctor, because he was a Jew.

He carried this feeling to such length, said the wife, that when they were married he said to her: "I don't want to interfere between you and any of your friends. But I simply cannot allow Jews to come into my home, even though they may be your old college classmates. If you accept invitations to their parties, you must understand that there will be no return invitations for them to visit you here."

As the acquaintance developed, the woman wished the Jewish doctor and her husband to become acquainted. She made several appointments, but always the husband was unable to appear or asked to have the meeting postponed.

When the services were ended and the woman was saying goodbye she said to the Jew:

"I want to tell you why my husband never would keep his appointments to meet you. He had heard enough to think you were a very nice fellow. He felt sure that if he met you, he would like you. If he called at your office, he would want to invite you to his home. And he would not let himself get in that position. He wanted to hold on to his prejudice."

The general public follows such blind prejudice in business when it walks past a store without considering the wares, because the name is Jewish.

When Jewish capitalists buy a Gentile business, the old name is retained, but seldom is it true in the reverse. And Jewish business men who have been handicapped by their own names will take in a foreman or a salesman as nominal partner, the business becoming known as Feinstein & Anderson, or O'Farrell & Co., while ownership remains exclusively Jewish. It is a well-recognized custom of all mail order businesses to sign correspondence with a familiar English name. Jackson and Smith are popular. They are supposed to inspire more confidence than would Jacobson or Rosenstein, or even Swenson.

Such transitions occur not without the play of humor. A salesman by the name of Solomon, having changed his name to Stevens, desired still to hold on to his old business. And so he sent around to all his customers a copy of the court authorization, with a letter beginning:

> " 'What's in a name?' said Bill Shakespeare, and so 'says ME.'
>
> "Anyway, mine has been changed to Stevens by court order, as the enclosed legalistic copy attests. The point is this—

> I haven't changed a bit, even if my name has. And I am still selling."

The *American Hebrew,* a few years ago, in innocence and good will included in its annual Jewish roll of honor the name of an artist who had done original and charming work.

Imagine the embarrassment of that magazine when the favored artist announced to the press of the world that he had been insulted and intended to bring suit for damages. It happened that a member of the *American Hebrew's* staff had lived as a boy in the same *Judenstrasse* with the artist. He called on him in anxiety.

"I had to do it," said the artist. "I am just on the point of getting an important contract, and if they knew I was a Jew, they wouldn't have me."

* * *

One might attempt a poor jest at a serious matter by asking, "When is a Jew not a Jew?" One answer is "When he says he is not." Or "When he embraces Christian Science or Ethical Culture;" or "When he changes his name."

The most striking commentary upon this tendency, perhaps, is contained in the preface to the first edition of "*Who's Who in American Jewry*" (1926), which says:

> "Doubtless many names have been omit-

> ted which should have been included. . . . Unfortunately, some persons preferred to be omitted rather than associate their names with those of their racial colleagues. A few even rejected with indignation the proposal of being included in a volume where their Jewish identity would become a matter of public knowledge."

New York City courts with their practically limitless fertility have provided a striking pair of exhibits in—perhaps—Americana Judaica. Everett Levy wanted his name changed to LeRoy and the gods assigned the case for hearing before Justice Aaron Levy. Louis Goldstein wanted his name changed to Golding, and his case was assigned to Justice Louis Goldstein. What would happen in cases such as that, even though a Daniel were come to judgment?

Said Justice Levy:

> "Character and courage are essential in fighting off these vicious and bigoted influences, but, as he prefers to run, let him. Doubtless he is wholly ignorant of the fact that the Bible tells us that the tribe of Levi never worshipped the Golden Calf. Let his application be granted, so that his people may be well rid of him."

Said Justice Goldstein:

> "The reasons advanced in the petition are that the name 'Goldstein' is not euphonious and un-American. . . . The court believes that the request of this petitioner is a subterfuge for the purpose of covering his religious and racial identity. . . . I am opposed to granting a change of name on such flimsy reasons as advanced in this petition."

Walter Winchell wrote in his column, "There is a warbler named May Le Veay, which is another way of spelling it."

The great American case of a change of name, however, was that of the family Kabotchnick, resident in Philadelphia. In spite of court action by the family Cabot, bluest of New England blue stockings, the Kabotchnicks were permitted also to become Cabots. Which provoked, in parody:

> *"Then here's to the city of Boston,*
> *The town of the cries and the groans,*
> *Where the Cabots can't see the Kabotchnicks*
> *And the Lowells won't speak to the Cohns."*

If age and length of tradition were the sole title to social distinction, the Jews probably would rank as the most aristocratic people on earth today. They certainly would make the Mayflower descendants appear no more than nouveaux riches. Some Jewish families in America can trace their ancestry back in authentic tradition to the Babylonian captivity. In many of these Jewish strains which have followed the rabbinical tradition from father to son, there is a direct line of nearly one hundred generations—all devoted to benevolence and learning.

And what avails the august race?

In the Manhattan telephone book there are five closely-set pages of Cohens and three pages of Levys. Neither name occurs even once in the New York Social Register.

Chapter X

JEWS AND JEWS

A CERTAIN number of discriminations which come up in cases of white collar workers may be attributable to factors not necessarily connected directly with race or religion. Young women aspiring to positions in the business world still hear very frequently in school, in the columns of various newspaper commentators, that business is business. I remember seeing recently an article by a well-known woman writer in which business girls were urged never to use rouge, or powder during office hours, and rigorously to exclude finery from their costumes. The point was that the worth of a woman in this fiercely competitive industrial age depended wholly upon sheer ability, and that feminine allurement was decidedly a handicap. Of course, this is utter nonsense. The average business man wants to have an office force which looks snappy. Even if he never puts this theory into words he will put it into practice.

There are, of course, just as many alluring young Jewish office workers as Gentile competitors. But to a certain extent the Jewish applicant may come from a group not long in this country. Her training in business school may represent the extreme sacrifice of a poor family which has not yet moved far on the road toward financial successes. The shops in her particular community may be of an inferior kind. She is somewhat less likely to have the same training and background in choice of clothes as comes to a New York girl of older antecedents in the community. Moreover, certain tastes in color combinations and effects can be grounded in a subconscious memory of a Russian or Roumanian village where it was considered well to be both neat and gaudy. These particular Slavonic tastes can be, from the point of view of the artist, more satisfactory than the somewhat duller conventions established by American civilization. I think there is no doubt that something alien to the eye of the average American Babbit is present in the general ensemble of at least a certain number of Jewish job-seekers.

It is well to remember that at least a certain portion of what we call anti-Jewish feeling is, in reality, a part of that vast suspicion which surrounds the foreigner in all lands. He is different, and we fear the thing with which we are not familiar. I know, of course, that part of the Jewish community is deeply rooted in native soil. The Spanish and the Portuguese groups are among the oldest New York families. There was a Jewish immigration to New York in the days of Peter Stuyvesant. The second oldest congregation in the city is Jewish, and still proudly displays the millstone which was part of their first synagogue.

Most of the German Jews can trace their American ancestry back for more than half a century. The Russian and the Roumanian influx is more recent. Some part of discrimination and diffidence which we call anti-Jewish, is in reality anti-Russian, anti-Roumanian, and applies in some measure to the Gentiles from these lands as well as to the Jews.

But getting back to the question of employment, a high official of a large department store which is wholly owned by Jewish capital said, "Yes, we have a quota on Jewish help for two reasons. Although we are Jewish owned, we do not desire to be known as a 'Jew store' and fear to become such in reputation if we have too many Jewish sales people; secondly, we do not want our staff too much depleted on the religious holidays." It may be that in some minds the adjective "Jewish" connotes a cut-rate establishment, or a place where there is the potentiality of haggling over a price. The mind, in its swift and far-flung forays, may go back to jokes and songs which were once associated with Bowery establishments and the puller-in who seized customers from the sidewalk and made them accept shoddy goods whether they would or not. Of course, there is no logic in this attitude. With very few exceptions the finest, and for that matter, most expensive of New York department stores are operated by Jews.

But logic is only a small component in the mind of any man or woman.

Here is a quotation from an article by Hugo K. Kessler, manager of the Efficiency Employment Exchange, 1452 Broadway, himself a Jew, published in *The Day,* November 3, 1929:

> "It is nothing unusual for a Jewish firm to call on us for Christian help. That is almost a daily occurrence with us.
>
> "I know Jewish men of prominence who control and operate million-dollar concerns, who are great philanthropists, who contribute thousands to Jewish orphanages and other Jewish charitable institutions. These very men have hundreds and in some cases thousands of people in their employ.
>
> "As a rule these companies have a personnel manager who is in control of all the engagement of help. In most of these cases the employment manager is a Gentile. We get calls from these very men almost daily and invariably they desire Christians. Where the concern has no personnel manager, each department head engages his own help. We find that most of these departments are headed by Christian executives, and they as a general rule also insist upon Christian help.

"These are not rare cases. I could name many. Here is the alarming part of it all. These very philanthropists who are devoting their expensive time and vast sums to aid Jewish charities and to uphold Jewry are overlooking what is going on under their own eyes."

The manager of a big employment agency told me this story:

"One of several Jewish partners who conducted a bank over in the Jewish section of the East Side asked me for an experienced banking man, to sit at a desk as an official of the bank and give personal service to customers. He must be Irish.

" 'Why don't you take a Jewish fellow?' I asked.

" 'No, no, our people would rather have an Irishman. They would rather deal with him, would have more confidence in him.'

"So we got him an Irishman, whom we can call O'Toole.

"I happened to be over in that neighborhood a couple of months later and stopped into the bank. Two of the partners were sitting at their desks, idle, while a line of East Side Jewish people waited to get up to

Mr. O'Toole's desk. One of the partners recognized an acquaintance in the line and said, 'Come right over here, Mr. Kaplan, I'll wait on you and you can save time.'

" 'Never mind,' answered Mr. Kaplan. 'I'll just wait for Mr. O'Toole.' "

* * *

As I have said, the Jews also have their parallel to the "Mayflower" social tradition, and it is altogether probable that Jacob Barsimson, the first recorded Jew in New York, who arrived from Holland on the *Pereboom,* may have felt somewhat superior to his co-religionists who followed a few weeks later on the *St. Charles.* The rule that the first-arrived assumes the air of aristocracy in contemplating the late comer holds true in the social classification of Jews in America.

Jews who trace back to that *Pereboom* and *St. Charles* period, the Spanish and Portuguese Jews who were so nearly the entire Hebraic population for a century and more, are the aristocracy of their race in America. Negligible in numbers, generally wealthy, having outgrown strife for position and recognition, for the most part they mix but slightly with the later immigrants. Intermarriage is not desired.

From these top strata, social rank in American Jewry grades down through the German Jews, the

Russians to the Galicians. Among the Germans, there is an internal division between Bavarians and those from over toward the Polish border, called in derision "Pollacks". Between Russian and Polish Jews there is little difference in the eyes of the outside, both having lived for long under the same flag, but the Russian is inclined to arrogate to himself a certain superiority. The Roumanians generally are on the same level with the Russians, having fled from Russia to Roumania during the same persecutions which produced the great emigration to America. The Galician, from the corner between Russia, Poland and Austria, being snubbed by the dominant Russians, often seeks refuge from the stigma by turning to the original sovereignty of his territory and announcing himself as Austrian.

A somewhat similar division exists, also, between the Jews in New York and those outside. Jews in the South and West, who generally suffer less discrimination in their communities, often resent the East Side Jew. They do not particularly welcome him when he comes into their territory, fleeing discrimination. "New York Jew" on the outside is no term of flattery.

Such intra-racial distinctions and rivalries, of course, serve only to emphasize the tendency of the human mind toward prejudice and the erection of artificial barriers. These divisions are the same as produce ill-feeling between Irish and English, between Norwegians and Swedes, which make groups of Americans refer to one another as "trifling Southerners" and "damned Yankees".

The divisions here suggested are only a few of the internal currents which press upon Jews in addition to the general offensive from outside directed at the race as a whole. Discriminations within are numerous and bitter. They are social and political, however, rather than economic.

In Jewish philanthropy, social service and foreign relief, rivalries center in the main between the Germans and the Russians. Although the German Jews are outnumbered twelve or fifteen to one by the Russians, they have the advantage of old-establishment, prestige, and wealth. And at present, Jewish community activities in general are directed and headed by the Germans.

* * *

Just as Jews deny their Jewishness and change their names to those of a Gentile sound, so within the ranks one finds Russian Jews who say they are Germans. This happens often about the time they forsake orthodoxy and join one of the reformed Jewish congregations. In many Russian Jewish families, it is considered a step upward in the world for a son or daughter to marry into a German Jewish family, while Russian parents do not encourage their children to stray toward the Galician young people.

On the other hand, some Russian Jews resent the sometimes flaunted airs of the Germans. Recently in New York, a Russian Jew, for many years chairman of an important committee in a philanthropic enterprise, had decided to retire. Learning then that a German was slated to succeed him, he refused to give up the place.

The story is told that when the Russian Jewish immigration was just reaching its tidal wave proportions about forty years ago, the newcomers proposed for the first time to establish a Yiddish theatre in New York. When the project became known, a German Jew bought up the property and refused to let it be used for the Yiddish drama.

This antagonism and social discrimination occurs noticeably in the Jewish Clubs. Some of the older, wealthier and more aristocratic Jewish clubs in New York, and other cities as well, have been operated for years on an exclusively German basis. Some of the clubs themselves have unintentionally defeated their own policies by building new club buildings so large and expensive that additional members had to be taken in, the result being an influx of Russians.

Certain golf clubs draw the line against orthodox Jews, permitting no one to join who is not a member of a reformed temple. A third generation American Jew, back-balling a recently arrived, prosperous Russian, remarked,

"A man with an accent can't play golf."

Many Gentiles justify their prejudice against Jews by saying, "Why, this exists among the Jews themselves." And there is no doubt of the tendency of certain people to criticize severely their own co-religionists. They do not criticize them perhaps under the name "Jews". But the word "kike" is fairly familiar in the vocabulary of the arrived and successful. I remember a friend of mine speaking of a mountain resort to which he used to go and saying, "Well, it was a nice place until so many kikes came there."

Undeniably some of the most contemptuous and fiercest prejudice has been visited upon the nouveau riche Jew by his fellows who are older in the attainment of success and fortune. As yet, there has been small disposition toward race or religious solidarity in the matter of persecution.

In so far as charity goes, the rich and influential Jew is good to his own. He will subscribe money to help the down-and-outer among his own people. But he is much less ready to extend the social hand of fellowship to those who have just emerged from below the surface of fierce economic struggle. Among the leaders in New York affairs are many Jews who have taken over much of the familiar Gentile jargon in regard to the nascent graduate of the Ghetto.

Chapter XI

THE WAY OUT

ANY discussion of the way out involves a vast problem. It would require the mind of a philosopher, psychologist, statistician, and prophet. Because after all, prejudice is a phase of hatred. To talk of abolishing all hatred is a man-sized order. The best I can do is to offer a certain number of surmises and, possibly, a suggestion or so.

This problem of race prejudice, which I admit is difficult, may also, from one point of view, be called extremely easy. There are no physical facts such as wind, weather, and mountain ranges to prevent everybody in the world's waking up at nine o'clock next Monday morning believing utterly in the theory that all men are created free and equal. We have carried that phrase along in oratory and in the essays of our country for more than a century. It is radical doctrine. It is a high aspiration. And yet I think its vitality means that it is not altogether a cerebration of the fantastic. Each one of us has felt the full force of it at some special period of his life and then slumped back again.

It is well to point out that race or religious prejudice is a restless state of mind. For instance, it might be quite simple to blow up Jewish prejudice if there was suddenly a large influx of Mohammedans into America. It has been remarked by many people that Californians at one time carried on a terrific anti-Chinese campaign, only to drop the greater part of it as soon as there were Japanese upon whom the community venom could be placed. And the Klan was in some sections of the country anti-Catholic, in others anti-Jewish, and in others anti-Negro. It is hard to hate too many groups at the same time.

But I am thinking of something a little better than a mere shifting of the burden. Some of the radical leaders insist that all prejudice has an economic basis. I have been told by certain of my Communist friends that just as soon as we adopt the principles of Soviet Russia all discrimination and prejudice will vanish. I don't share this view. Even if I believed in the technique of Communism I should still have a fear that some elements of disaffection would remain, even under the dictatorship of the proletariat.

In theory one might take an entirely opposite attitude, and assert that the cure could come from an extension of spiritual interests, rather than the triumph of a materialistic philosophy. It is perfectly true that according to the letter of Christian belief one is exhorted to love his neighbor as oneself, and in spite of a few exceptions raised now and then by fundamentalist pastors, I have no reason to believe that this injunction was not intended to include everybody. Still, whatever hope may lie in the growth of our familiar religions, it must be admitted that the Christian Church, as we know it, is a pretty bad bet as a healing force. It has had its chance for centuries, and nobody can possibly contend that it's been effective in easing prejudice or discouraging discrimination.

Those things can be changed by changing mass thinking. It may be objected that when I say there is no physical barrier like a mountain, I am putting in its place something even more solidly anchored. It may be more difficult to move the mind of millions than to move a mountain. Faith will move a mountain. It hasn't dislodged prejudice. But I think education could. And maybe education will. Don't interrupt to say that after all some of the most bitter facts of prejudice exist in our colleges and universities which are supposedly the centres of culture and learning. You know as well as I do that there is much in any far-reaching educational scheme transcending the best which colleges have to offer. I think I have seen the words of a man who may prove to be a Messiah in the matter of cleansing the world from racial hatreds. After the traditions of Messiahs he is, himself, a Jew. Dr. Sigmund Freud has opened the eyes of the modern world to those vast and unexplored continents of the unconscious.

And it is in these lands we shall find the root and kernel of prejudice. We must get under the surface if we are to end group hatreds.

I am aware that Dr. Freud, himself, has never envisaged a world without hatred. It is, in the eyes of every analyst, a necessary and heartening force in human conduct. But there is no great potentiality of invigoration in hating a race or a group. A Catholic priest once wrote me a letter taking issue with my somewhat vague mysticism, and said that no man could ever love anything save some object around which he could put his arms. He went on to explain that that was why it was useful to personify the saviour as a child. And, likewise, I think that any healthy hate must be directed against an individual, not a whole mass of people. You can only hate the thing which you can actually punch in the nose.

The difficulty of arguing people out of race prejudice is that few of them know the cause by which they are animated. James Harvey Robinson once said that all men live by two sets of reasons—good reasons and true reasons. In other words, if I say I don't like Jim Jones because he once played a hand very badly when I was his partner in a bridge game, I am giving a spurious reason for my dislike, even if it sounds fairly logical. Under an analysis it may turn out that at the age of two or three I was frightened by a red-haired man and Jim Jones has red hair. Even if he played the hand perfectly I still wouldn't have liked him. And in the same way the man who tells me, "I don't like Jews because I have met a number who were uncouth and vulgar," is not actually revealing his true motivation.

I cannot qualify as a mass psycho-analyst or any other kind. But I will venture to wager that in practically every case some incident or train of incidents may be discovered which will serve as an explanation, and all these incidents would come out of childhood. I think that one of the most familiar is the influence of church or Sunday School. It is true that most religious bodies have recently tried to remove from their texts any definite assertion to the children that the Jews killed Christ. But it need not be pointed. The Bible story itself cannot fail to put some such notion in the head of the child. Things over which the teacher slides quickly may be the very things which take hold.

I can remember somewhat irrelevantly that I was brought up in a congregation which rather sedulously refrained from emphasizing hell-fire, and yet in my teens I spent a horrible year of agony and anguish, thinking and trembling about hell.

We shall have to have for our Utopia a race of people trained always to get to the source of emotions. This will disturb many concepts. Much which we reverence and hold dear would go by the boards, and yet if it served to eliminate prejudice and discrimination I can think of nothing which I, personally, would not throw into the depths of the ocean.

* * *

I have said that some phases of Jewish prejudice are associated with a very deep-seated kind of suspicion and fear which all people have for the foreigner. In our childhood, at least, the thing which is in any way strange is of necessity fearsome. Even an accent has an alienating quality.

But as the years roll on it is obvious that the greater number of Jewish inhabitants of America are in no way strange. It is not possible to identify any large proportion of the millions as members of this or that religious group. It may be presumptuous for me to state the opinion that in a not-too-slow process of assimilation the Jew as "a Jew" may disappear. I am aware that this is a happening which would seem tragic to practically every Jewish leader. I am not denying that it would have tragic implications. And, of course, I may be entirely wrong. The fact will be presented that for almost two thousand years in many quarters of the globe, the Jewish group has retained its identity, but this has been partly conditioned by pressure from the outside.

We had the spectacle of a proud people and a people animated by a highly developed culture and a highly developed religion. That gives you something with which to hold your stones together. But remember that in addition there came discrimination, regulation, even laws assigning a place of residence.

With all its faults of passion and prejudice, it can hardly be said that in America any Jew is definitely forced into a pale or Ghetto. In college I observed that almost every student came out at the end of four years much less firm in a dogmatic religious belief, even though he had one when he entered. And, naturally enough, that loosening of the bonds between the boy in the Baptist Church or Catholic Church was equally present in regard to the Jew and the orthodox synagogue.

Orthodoxy of any kind is difficult under modern conditions. It was much easier to have a Puritan Sabbath in a pioneer country where industrialism was slightly developed. It is easier to let a cornfield shift for itself for a single day than it is to close down a coal mine or a subway system for an equal length of time. And, obviously, Jewish orthodoxy was framed to suit the needs and requirements of a pastoral people. The electric refrigerator, for one thing, takes a good deal of logic out of dietary regulations. And only the most devout Jews are able to follow literally the complicated customs of their faith when living in a large American city.

In this connection it may be pertinent to quote a few lines from *Folkways* of William Graham Sumner, who wrote:

"The real reason for the hatred of Jews

> by Christians has always been the strange and foreign *mores* of the former. When Jews conform to the *mores* of the people amongst whom they live, prejudice and hatred are gradually diminished and in time will probably disappear."

And in another point in his book Professor Sumner said:

> "In the rabbinical period, the Jews emphasized everything which could distinguish them from the heathen."

I also have in mind a certain uneasiness which may arise even in the mind of an unorthodox Jew against the rigors and complications of elaborate ritual. A friend of mine whose family had been mild agnostics for two or three generations, although purely Jewish in racial stock, married a young girl who was deeply devout. He used to describe to me the irritation which he felt at the detail of the observance which was necessary in his own home on religious festivals, and in connection with Sabbath regulation. It isn't altogether easy to adapt yourself to a form which prescribes no lighting of fires except by a hired outlander, no carrying of keys or currency, no tearing of paper.

* * *

Naturally, it is not my function to assail the validity of religious custom, either Jewish or Gentile. I am perfectly ready to admit that fidelity to religion has been a preservative for the integrity of the Jewish race. But it is only fair to say that anybody who bridles against certain dogmatic rules of Christian ritual will, in all logic, have the same personal impatience with what seems to me an overlay of the outward manifestation of love for God. There is, at least, a hint of some common meeting ground in the rapid development of modernism in both faiths. It is, of course, a wrench for any Jew to break tradition to the extent of joining a Catholic, a Baptist, or a Methodist congregation. Indeed, there is reason for the suspicion that such steps are often actuated by reasons far removed from religious conviction.

A discussion of the graduations which separate the most orthodox synagogue in New York from the extreme reform school would require the heavy labor of a profound scholar. It should be enough to indicate that the process goes step by step, and that a Jew may move quite gradually away from complete orthodoxy. In fact, even those congregations most faithful to tradition have known some changes down through the centuries. Judaism, like every other religion, has had its Luthers.

Moreover, it is well to remember that the system of church government is congregational. A heresy trial would be all but impossible. Each congregation chooses its own rabbi without let or hindrance. And, generally speaking, he is directly responsible to no one else.

However, Spinoza was excommunicated by the Jewish community of Amsterdam and upon his tomb was written the phrase of double insult, "Here lies Spinoza, Jew and Atheist."

From the most extreme reformed congregation to any so-called Christian sect a Jew must make something of a leap. But the chasm can be bridged. Unitarianism is a ready refuge. For instance. Dr. John Haynes Holmes, of the Community Church, says that half of his congregation is Jewish. It is easy to understand this, because the sticking point is not to any great degree Christian ethics, but the divinity of Jesus. After all if the persecutions of Jews in all parts of the world rest, to some extent, upon the Biblical story of His crucifixion at the instigation of the Jews, it is only fair to say that the Jews have likewise been crucified by the world in His name. It is no great wrench for a Jew to accept Christ as a teacher, or even as one of the prophets. After all, he was distinctly a product of Judaism, and his ethical teachings did not necessarily war with those of the older leaders. It is a mistake to assume, as many clergymen do, that New Testament thought makes a complete right-about-face from the Old Testament. No leader of Jewish thought today is pounding home a literal eye-for-an-eye theory.

Neighborly love and good will to all is a doctrine equally acceptable to Jew and Gentile.

But it is asking much to expect any Jew with an emotional grounding in his own faith to give up the hope of a promised messiah in favor of one who has seemed, in the light of church development, to be a redeemer for Gentiles alone. I am aware that this was hardly the purport of Christ's mission as he expressed it himself. But it has been twisted about to such an extent that every now and then some little boy in a Baptist or Methodist Sunday School is shocked and horrified if anybody points out to him the fact that Jesus was a Jew.

The particular item in orthodoxy which has exposed Jews to the greatest amount of ridicule is, unquestionably, the prohibition of pork. The ham anecdote is ancient and prolific. For years it served as a sort of *shibboleth* by which the alien could be identified. I wonder why we have all been so passionate about pork. The fact that a Jew refuses ham tended, for some inexplicable reason, to make some people very angry. It would almost seem as if we were a nation of packers. And yet, when some nature cult arises and bans pork, or possibly all meat, we may think it curious but it doesn't annoy us. As a matter of fact, this particular bit of orthodoxy is breaking down rapidly. Some members of reformed congregations more or less make a point of eating ham publicly in order to show their indifference toward an ancient taboo.

But emotionalism is a curious thing. A friend of mine said, "Yes, I eat ham. I see no reason why I shouldn't. I have no logical faith in any religious reason for my abstaining, and yet when I eat it, it makes me a little sick." There you have the unconscious fidelity to a faith which is so common in the case of many stragglers away from all kinds of orthodoxy. The offices of neurologists are filled with patients who have thought themselves out of the Catholic Church, but never quite felt their way out. It may be that this same phenomenon is familiar in the case of the orthodox Jew, who moves by solely mental processes to the religious left-wing. Christian Science has taken over a number of Jews. Here there is no denial of the divinity of Christ, but from a theological standpoint I assume that the trinitarian concept is lessened by the position of Mrs. Eddy in the cosmic scheme. The Episcopal Church also has its converts in spite of its fundamentalist character insofar as a literal Son of God is concerned. I rather suspect that Episcopalianism represents, not so much religious, as social security for the convert.

Another movement which may well provide a common meeting ground for Gentiles and Jews is Humanism, as preached by the Rev. Charles Francis Potter, which takes its ethics from the religious teachings of many faiths and makes no demand of belief in the supernatural. And, of course, the Ethical Culture movement has been another effort to combine Judaism and Christianity, retaining the best features of each.

The moot subject of Zionism offers, in a measure, a way out. Curiously enough, this movement should be enthusiastically accepted by prejudiced Gentiles. After all, it is an effort to preserve a Jewish Homeland, to give a national reputation to the Jew. But I don't assume that even the most ardent Zionist has ever thought it possible, or desirable, to make Palestine the literal home of all the Jews of the world. Its position in Jewish thought is rather more romantic than anything else. I have spoken of the possibility of a more complete assimilation in America. Possibly Zionism doesn't war against this concept, since the existence of a Sweden and a Norway has not halted the rapid assimilation of the Scandinavian in the middle west, nor has Irish assimilation been stopped by the creation of a Free State.

* * *

Occasionally, a very minor point in an alien ritual will do much to arouse terrific antagonism. I remember on one occasion I was scheduled to speak at an orthodox synagogue. The other half of the program was to be occupied by a young Jewish violinist. His was a name very favorably known in the community, and so we had a much larger turnout than expected. In order to accommodate the audience it was necessary to use the synagogue itself rather than the basement hall which was reserved for secular activities. The assistant rabbi said to me, "You won't mind talking with your hat on." I knew of the custom and it aroused no resentment in me, although possibly I had a slight feeling of looking a little foolish since I was not used to lecturing from under a derby. Just as we were about to begin, the accompanyist of the violinist arrived. He was non-Jewish. When informed that he would be expected to play the piano with his head covered, he became exceedingly angry and began to shout, "Play with my hat on? I should say not!" In high dudgeon he went away, and I must admit that the graceless nature of his prejudice bore heavily on me. Since the young violinist could not play without an accompanist, I had to make my talk twice as long, and revive four ancient anecdotes which I had promised to abandon. Obviously, the young man who stalked out into the night rather than wear his hat while playing, was not traditionally anti-Jewish. He had worked on many occasions with the young violinist. They were friends. But one touch of alien custom is enough to make the whole world anything but kin.

I am told that in rural sections of North Carolina the word "Jew" is freely applied to any foreigner whose nationality is not closely identified. If a Greek opens a restaurant in a village, he is referred to by the inhabitants as a Jew regardless of his religious affiliations, and any Syrian peddler who passes by is also a Jew. The word in those sections simply means one who is not a native. He is a stranger and an alien.

I don't want to give the impression that I think there is any fairness in urging or encouraging a break from Jewish orthodoxy simply because it demands certain customs which are not convenient, in modern American city life. But I must confess that my own personal feeling is for an abatement of orthodoxy all the way around. I do feel that an enormous amount of friction is created by conflicting ritual. And if you tell me each man has a right to worship God in whatever form pleases him, I cannot very well deny the assertion. But for the sake of a kindly and companionate world, I could wish that ritual, whether Jewish or Gentile, could, at the very least, be confined to the edifice of worship, and not slopped over into the communal life outside. And, of course, I am actually maintaining the position of "a plague on both your houses."

I am, I must admit, one of the Gentiles who is faintly annoyed to find the tailor or the news dealer shut down upon an occasion which I do not anticipate. But I am equally, or even more indignant, if I happen to be in a city on a Sunday and find that because of the power of the Lord's Day Alliance, motion picture shows are not permitted, and the big league teams may not meet on the ball diamond.

If the end of prejudice lies in complete amalgamation there must be no barrier against intermarriage. Obviously, alliances between Jews and Gentiles are much more common than a century ago. The only significant handicap lies in religious orthodoxy. I speak now of the New York community where no great attention is aroused if a Gentile girl marries a Jewish young man, or the other way about. But we do shape prejudice in these matters in a curious way. The Jewish young woman who bears the children of a Gentile man, brings young Gentiles into the world. Within a generation nobody thinks of these boys or girls as Jewish. Of course, there is the factor that they bear a non-Jewish name. But I think it goes deeper than that. The children of the Jewish father by a Gentile wife remain Jewish in the eyes of the community, even to the fourth and fifth generation. I have known the descendants of a mixed marriage to suffer the usual and traditional discrimination, even though they were no more than one-fourth or one-eighth Jewish. I assume that this somewhat illogical process of thought rests upon the conception of the male as the master of the household, the head of the family, the person who determines its complexion. And, of course, it is true that marriage outside of the Jewish community has long been practiced by those people. This was true even in the earliest records. The Bible is filled with stories of the manner in which the Children of Israel took over the young women of a conquered tribe. But this family admixture was quickly absorbed. There are, of course, stories of the adoption of alien males, but at least one incident bears eloquent testimony that circumcision in itself did not make the stranger wholly acceptable to the conqueror.

Here we have an instance of the way in which a particular rite may be a symbol of clash and have all manner of irrelevant emotion built up around the custom. Thus there was the familiar phrase "uncircumcized dog", and a great deal of rather bitter humor came to rest upon the circumcized. One might well have believed a hundred years ago that a minor surgical operation actually altered the psychology or spiritual make-up of a man. But here we have a case in which a religious rite justified itself by becoming a medical recommendation. Circumcism is now almost a regular part of the procedure of any modern obstetrician, and at least one mark of difference tends to disappear.

There is also in this country, at least, a move toward physical conformity in the matter of the beard going out of fashion. Once upon a time the beard was a distinguishing mark of the devout Jew, and while it is true that this sign of orthodoxy is retained by some it certainly diminishes in moving up from the East side to West End or Riverside Drive. Very few Jews carry their beards with them.

And, by an obvious association of ideas, I might mention a play which has been extremely harmful in establishing race prejudice in the minds of school boys and girls. I know that many actors have eagerly assumed the role of Shylock, and have contended that the part is one of noble grandeur. It is also true that Shakespeare has given the Jew some stirring lines of protest against prejudice. And yet there can be little doubt that Shakespeare wrote for an audience which was almost entirely anti-Jewish. Since he was a genius he did have an intuitive recognition of things which went on in the heart of the character, but the eloquence of Shylock in anguish undoubtedly shot over the heads of an Elizabethan audience, just as today it shoots over the head of the pupil in high school or grammar school. He will not go away remembering:

> "Hath not a Jew eyes? Hath not a Jew hands, organs, dimensions, senses, affections, passions? Fed by the same food, hurt with the same weapons, subject to the same diseases, healed by the same means, warmed and cooled by the same winter and summer as a Christian is?"

He is more likely to be impressed with the fact that

Shylock is avaricious, revengeful, and cruel. At least these first two qualities fit in with popular fallacies, and it would be an excellent day's work to remove the "Merchant of Venice" from all schools and leave it as required reading only for mature students. I might add, impertinently, as far as I am concerned I would have it required reading for no one since I have always felt that in spite of undeniable fugitive beauty and dramatic effectiveness, the play remains among the poorest of Shakespeare's works.

* * *

The question whether Jewish culture is inseparably bound up in the Jewish religion presents a problem which is likely to find divergent answers. In the past, these two factors have been the mortar responsible for the entity of the Jewish community. At the same time there are a certain number of Jewish leaders who feel that even a great diminishment of orthodoxy in religion will, in no wise, impair the existence of the group.

To some extent, holy days of Judaism are celebrated by certain individuals less out of a convinced religious belief than as a testimonial of pride and affection for a people of long history and great achievement. This is not an unusual phenomenon. Some of the most ardent celebrants of Christmas within my acquaintance are men with no distinct belief in the divinity of Jesus. They merely like the romance and tradition of the day. It might be remarked here that Christmas has been distinctly the bone of contention among the Jews of large American cities. To the orthodox, it seems monstrous that any festivities should occur on a day in theory devoted to honoring the birth of a Messiah, a Messiah necessarily unacceptable to Jews. Yet, it is obvious that very many Jews have fallen in with their Gentile compatriots to mark Christmas as a good day for a big party, as an event for the giving of gifts, and a suitable occasion for sending out cards of greeting. In looking over my own batch of cards last year, I made a rough calculation that approximately forty per cent came from Jewish friends. This is a somewhat specific instance of what I mean in speaking of a common meeting place between the Jew and the Gentile. Certainly, among my own particular circle of non-Jewish friends, Christmas is a jolly and, practically wholly, secular day. There may be behind it, in many cases, dim childhood memories of church services, the odor of incense, and other fragments of recollection. But it distinctly is not a religious day in any dogmatic sense of the word.

There is, at the same time, the problem in regard to New Year's, where an acceptance of the calendar is, to some extent, a denial of Jewish chronology. It is my impression that in the case of this, obviously, the Jews have all the better of it, since many calmly, but not too calmly, celebrate two New Year's Eves each year.

I said in the beginning that any prediction of utter assimilation is presumptuous. Possibly, I may overestimate the factor of outside pressure. There have been communities here and there in which Jewish culture and Jewish religion were tolerated by a companionate people. Yet, in the long run, history seems to say that two groups do not live side by side unmixed in blood, unless there is a definite barrier of hostility.

It is difficult for me to accept the somewhat simple theory that it is all done by economics. Under a strict Americanized identification, you will find the Jewish group divided among the capitalist class, the bourgeoise, and the proletariat. Certainly, American civilization has not forced the Jew into any iron-clad economic position. Those who have studied history tell me that Jews became the bankers of the world largely out of necessity, and not from any inherent racial genius for finance. In some communities, orthodox Christianity made it sinful to charge interest on money, and this prohibition did not extend to the Jews. They were very generally shut off from the land. And it is only since the development of the Zionist movement that there has been a large scale attempt to get the Jew into farming. Of course, there have been a few Jewish farmers in America. But it is not for them a common occupation.

Some of my learned Jewish acquaintances are, I believe, a little sentimental and a little romantic about the necessity of a return to the early traditions of a pastoral people. I have known instructors, assistant professors, and even professors, to say that they would like to toss aside their learning, their prestige, their university followings, if only they could settle down to rear a grove of olives. On such occasions I shake my head doubtfully, for I, too, belong to a group in which there is much talk of the return to the farm and the glory of labor upon the land. Practically every newspaper reporter, at the end of a hard day's work, will weep into his beer and speak of the day in which he can leave it all for a little place up state or in New Hampshire, or Vermont. Yet, few ever make the fearful trip from the sidewalks of New York to the green hills. Of thousands I have known only one has done it. The others never will and do not, in their heart of hearts, desire such a transformation. And so I believe that the resumption of a pastoral life among the Jews of America will never occur upon any considerable scale.

* * *

For myself, I have never been able to identify that point of view which is sometimes called Jewish psychology. As one who studied, after a fashion, under Gentile and Jewish teachers, I am not aware that there was any marked differentiation between the approach which they indicated to their scholars. If there is a real difference in thinking, the gap closes rapidly. We all read the same magazines, the same books, and soon we will all subscribe to the same newspapers. There still exists a powerful Yiddish press. The *Vorwaerts* of New York is one of the most successful and influential papers in the country, for it circulates considerably beyond the borders of the state. But the gentlemen who control the destinies of the paper are aware of the fact that within an appreciable time their paper will have to become an English-language publication, and take on the general character of the American press. Already English sections have been introduced, once a week, and a fund has been provided against the day when the complete change will occur.

And, as a somewhat personal confirmation for my belief that psychological differences are slight, I may cite the fact that when I first lost my job on the *World,* I was offered a position to do a column for the *Vorwaerts,* although my previous newspaper connections had been entirely with the English press. I might add that the *Vorwaerts* did not require or contemplate my contributing in Yiddish, and it was not prejudice, but a previous contract, which made it impossible for me to accept the offer. I should like to have written for an exclusively Jewish public, because if I had tried that experiment I would be in a better position to prove my theory that the material which goes well enough for the Nordic, the semi-Nordic and the unorthodox Jew, will suffice to interest readers who are still strong in the faith of Israel.

It may be, then, that a way out would make fewer changes in habits and customs than I believe to be inevitable. And, lest I tread on anybody's toes and dogmas, I am not insisting that a whittling away from old-fashioned orthodoxy, both Jewish and Gentile, would be a good thing. It so happens that I, personally, am in favor of such a scaling down from all rigid formality. But I am trying to stress, not my wish, but the thing which I believe is bound to occur. And in that development my wish can neither stay or speed such a happening.

Even if there be no such day, a beginning of comradeship could be imminent. Friendship does not depend upon complete acceptance of the other fellow's faith or customs. It is a familiar joke in colleges—it was true in the Harvard of my day—that the Jewish student and the Irish Catholic were frequently found joined together in the intimacy of sharing two bedrooms and a study. The combination worked well. Both members of the firm felt that they were somewhat under the disfavor of Brahmin New England orthodoxy. They made common cause. If friendliness can arise out of the fact of pressure, it may even be that our present economic adversity will eventually bring about better understanding rather than greater discrimination.

It has been said, and I think it is undoubtedly true, that unemployment has heightened discrimination. This need not continue. If we ever gain the point of view that our industrial ills are world-wide in origin and soluble only by international cooperation, we may even see through to the fact that no group can be excluded from membership in the rescuing crew. We are very literally and truly in the same boat. We will have to get hold of oars and lock hands as we pull together. Since civilization has come to a point where sustenance itself can be won only after a battle against terrific risks—poverty, unemployment and illness—we might find close communion in the realization that each one of us is potentially outcast. We may not share common faith, a common cultural heritage, a common racial background. But there is just one life, and that we must share in common if we are to be able to maintain a finger-hold upon this flying sphere.

* * *

Naturally enough, there has been some suggestion that fire is the inevitable weapon against fire. In a recent sermon a Jewish member of the Columbia faculty advised his coreligionists to meet prejudice by building up an exclusiveness of their own. "Rear a new Jerusalem," he said, "within the walls of the college campus." Some development has been made along these lines. There are numerous golf courses around New York City in which membership is confined to Jews. And some of the most expensive and magnificent of New York clubs are Jewish. Mr. Walter Winchell is authority for the statement that there is a Jewish swimming pool in Elberon, New Jersey, which rigidly excludes all Gentiles. And the development may lead further into such schemes as the creation of a Jewish university and a Jewish medical school.

I am not of the opinion that there is much virtue in such a plan. After all, it has been tried in the past. Many of the powerful and influential Jews of an earlier day were proud and arrogant in their dealings with peoples who sought to discriminate against them. If there is to be any such large-scale movement, it will hardly result in achieving the democratic ideals of which we talk so freely. It will be setting up a separate community within the community. Also, it seems to me that most Jews in America are not inclined to enter into any such campaign of retaliation. I have heard numerous stories of censure visited upon some Gentile clubman because he took a Jewish friend to play over his golf course. The reverse is not true, even in country clubs which are established for Jewish members there is no disposition to say that a Gentile may not play a round now and again.

To a certain number of humorous and intelligent people there lies the remedy of treating the whole sorry scheme of discrimination as a joke. I am aware that any Freudian will identify this as defense mechanism. Yet, it is effective. For instance, I am thinking of the encounter between Harpo Marx and a well known Long Island resort. The comedian had telegraphed for accommodations, and when he arrived a clerk eyed him and made inquiry as to his religion. Mr. Marx's answer was to walk boldly to the register and sign Harpo MacMarx, which answered all objections and certainly made the hotel the butt in the incident.

I think that much might be done in a somewhat organized campaign to make fun of prejudice and show its ridiculous aspects. I am under the impression that the downfall, or at least, the diminishment of the power and influence of the Klu Klux Klan began with the tide of ridicule heaped upon it. Few young men were deterred from joining the organization when it was under serious and bitter attack. It seemed romantic and thrilling to belong to something which was held up as a menace and as a powerful factor in the creation of an invisible government. If an orator thundered denunciation and declared that state, and even national, elections were swayed by this white-robed order, many wanted to get in and belong to the ruling class. But there was less appeal after hundreds and thousands of cartoons had been drawn in which the Klansman was pictured as a fool rather than a menace. A white robe was one thing, and a nightshirt quite another.

I remember vividly a cartoon of Edmund Duffy's in the Baltimore *Sun*. This was drawn at a time when there was a vigorous campaign requiring the Klan to unmask. Mr. Duffy drew a picture of a Klansman who had complied with this request, and with the hood raised there was revealed a scraggly, meagre, chinless little fellow conceived in the mould of Mr. Common People who figures so much in American art. The caption was "Put it on again".

We have had a good many plays which undertook to point out the humors and the tragedies of race discrimination. It is really up to me to pay a belated tribute to *Abie's Irish Rose*. I was among the critics who saw this show at its first performance, and I remember I predicted it would not run a month. At the end of the first year I had to switch and take the stand that it wouldn't run forever. But for a long time it seemed possible that I might be wrong a second time. I am still aware of the fact that it was a cheaply conceived and crudely executed story, full of gross sentimentalism and standardized humour. All the stencils of the joke papers were included. There was even the comic Irishman who flew into a rage when offered oranges. And yet, in retrospect, I am not at all sure that *Abie's Irish Rose* did not more or less fulfill the function of *Uncle Tom's Cabin*. And that didn't happen to be a very good novel, either. The millions of people who saw the play and enjoyed it so much, must have come away with a feeling that race prejudice was cruel and that race prejudice was comic. It was a bad play. But it was a superb piece of propaganda, and to me it indicates that there is a longing in the hearts of Jews and of Gentiles to be rid of the cumbersomeness of prejudices.

Another very successful Jewish comedy, or rather, series of comedies, was written by Montague Glass around the characters of Potash and Perlmutter. They were in the cloak and suit business and later, for the sake of plot, became motion picture magnates.

Mr. Glass wrote with keen insight and humor, and the incidents of the plays took up a good many of the surface characteristics of some phases in the lives of some Jews which are used in the explanations of those who justify Jewish prejudice. Potash and Perlmutter were presented as vulgar, grasping, and tricky in small detail. But each play ended on the note that these were merely minor manifestations, and that underneath it all the characters were people of generosity and fineness in any true pinch. Seemingly this compromise attitude was satisfactory to Jewish audiences which supported the plays largely. And it might be well to add that only in the case of the grossest and cruelest sort of caricature has there been Jewish protest against racial jokes.

Unlike the Irish, for instance, the Jewish sense of humour is receptive even to quips aimed at and around Jews. Here, of course, you do encounter the whole subject of defensive mechanism. The Jew who tells Jewish stories is a familiar type. But there may be some reason to suspect that he retails these anecdotes himself to forestall some Gentile who may bring up the same witticisms in a more stinging way.

It is distressing to be discriminated against. And in time it becomes a bore and a nuisance to discriminate. It makes life so much more complex. No prejudice can be maintained unless both sides are constantly on guard. You have to have your picket lines and your outposts and sentries.

My own feeling about prejudice, I am sure, is not merely an identification which I make with any put-upon group on account of my own inferiority complex. It is more involved than that. It has something to do with my inherent laziness. After all, only active and energetic people can maintain prejudice. It's so much simpler to sit back and say "Oh, what the hell." And I must maintain that in addition to being simpler, it is also more sensible.